# YOU'RE WHAT?!

## Survival Strategies for
## Straight Spouses

# YOU'RE WHAT?!

## Survival Strategies for
## Straight Spouses

Heather Cram

Bascom Hill Publishing

Bascom Hill Publishing Group
212 3rd Avenue North, Suite 570
Minneapolis, MN 55401
612.455.2293
www.bascomhillpublishing.com

ISBN - 978-0-9802455-8-5
ISBN - 0-9802455-8-3
LCCN - 2008932128


Book sales for North America and international:
Itasca Books, 3501 Highway 100 South, Suite 220
Minneapolis, MN 55416
Phone: 952.345.4488 (toll free 1.800.901.3480)
Fax: 952.920.0541; email to orders@itascabooks.com


Cover Design by Alan Pranke
Typeset by Tiffany Laschinger


Printed in the United States of America

# Contents

# This book is dedicated to:

My mom and dad, brother and sister, and friends who give unwavering daily support to me and to my children. It is through their consistent caring and love that I survived the events that occurred before, during, and after my husband "came out" in my marriage.

Jackie, Mary and Carol for allowing me to tell their stories. I applaud them for their courage in exposing their truths to help others.

Millions of straight women worldwide who become members of a secret sisterhood when they discover their husbands are gay.

The father of my children, who walks beside me in raising them to be tolerant, loving human beings.

# INTRODUCTION

After 14 years in a happy marriage I found out that my husband was gay. It shook my world and that of my children, who were 11 and 8 at the time. I never saw it coming and sometimes, looking back, I still can't believe the whole thing happened. In a moment I went from being a happy, lighthearted, healthy, loving mother and wife of a handsome straight man to an angry, confused, terrified, lonely, unhealthy single mom, divorced from a gay man. My large suburban home with a pool and a landscaper turned into a tiny domicile with a detached garage and a new landscaper – me. The gregarious, busy mother who was known for organizing birthday parties and play dates disappeared behind a wall of shame, fear and doubt. A good marriage (at least I thought it was good) turned into a divorce mired in angst and loathing and bitterness and confusion. As my children shuffled between old houses, new houses and apartments, their grades suffered, their self esteem nosedived and their anxiety levels skyrocketed.

It has been a very long road back to creating sanity for me, my kids, their dad and our newly designed family. We are coping every moment. Most days, finally, are pretty good, though there are still many hard times. Each of these days, good or bad, we are still learning to deal successfully with a difficult situation. We are managing the twists and turns of our new lives...hopefully moving toward our goal of a peaceable, happy existence. I was able to survive the catastrophic events that occur when a spouse changes sexual orientation mostly because I had a wide and loving support network. And because, as I have come to find out, I'm a heck of a lot tougher than I thought I could be.

'Coming out' in marriage is a growing phenomenon. Thanks to increasing media exposure through movies such as "Brokeback Mountain" and topical shows like Oprah and The Ellen Degeneres Show, large numbers of gay or bisexual spouses in heterosexual marriages are disclosing their same-sex attractions or activities. Some will wait until the children are grown. Some will wait until they are in a committed relationship outside their marriage. Some, very unfortunately, never will disclose that they are gay. Whenever it happens, we as spouses are devastated by the confession.

This book was written for the millions of women worldwide who are married to gay men. Some of you know that your spouse is gay. Some of you have a sneaking suspicion. Some of you have no idea yet. Many of you feel isolated and alone. You are embarrassed by your situations. In most cases, you had no idea that your husband was gay before you married him. You probably did not believe that gay men even married straight women. I am here to tell you that they do!

Here is the truth: gay men live out in the open and they are hidden behind closed doors. They are successful businessmen in suits and construction workers and doctors delivering babies. They are husbands and fathers and politicians and coal miners.

Many of you reading this book believe you have something to do with your husband's homosexuality. Many of you have felt a loss of self-esteem and a loss of sexuality. I felt it, too. After I found out that my husband was gay, I fell into a pretty dark place. All my conventional hopes and dreams and expectations for my family vanished in a moment.

Immediately after I found out about my husband's change in sexual identity, I bought every book available on the subject. Bonnie Kaye's book "Straight Wives: Shattered Lives" became my bible. In that book,

27 women tell their stories of life before, during and after they realized they were "straight wives." Carol Grever's book "My Husband Is Gay," which also is a conglomeration of women's experiences, was helpful as well. My copies of both books have dog-eared pages and big red circles around women's stories that were like mine! For months I searched the internet for clues about how to deal with my difficult situation. I was amazed at the limited amount of information I was able to find: a few books, a handful of magazine articles and just a few support groups. In fact, my research showed very little media exposure about what to do if your husband comes out in your marriage.

As a bit of a women's advocate, I am angry about the way we (straight wives of gay husbands) have been relatively ignored by the media. After watching "Brokeback Mountain" at a movie theatre I felt sick to my stomach. Everyone was talking about the "poor guys who had to hide their sexuality." What about the loving wives who are left behind to pick up the pieces of the family and try to make sense of it all? What about the loneliness and isolation of the women who are devastated by the unexpected loss of their trust and the lives they thought they had? What about the women whose husbands had secret liaisons before coming out? They get tested for STDs and AIDS and wait nervously for the results. We can't imagine why our husbands, who loved us, put us at risk for all kinds of diseases – some fatal – and put our children at risk of becoming orphans.

The devastating impact of gay liberation on the lives of straight wives is harrowing. Most spouses like us endure our pain in silence, on our side of the closet, while our gay or bisexual partners find support from their established "communities." The coming out creates incredible trauma for spouses. We feel shocked and rejected sexually. We are lonely and grieving for the mates we thought we had.

It seems like the media, until very recently, has been skipping over the plight of straight wives because it is not sensational or alluring or sexy. We are often ignored yet must overcome great adversity and despair; we are forced to readjust our lives alone, in private. While there are many support networks for gay men coming to terms with their homosexuality, there are limited resources for women who are left behind to deal with the aftermath.

I am one of the women who the media left behind. I was blindsided by my husband's change in sexual orientation. My family blew up and my world grew dark. I lost my job and I lost my house. I lost my self-worth and I questioned my faith. I lost a great deal of my money paying for therapists and lawyers and health insurance. And I was one of the lucky ones.

Given the unexpected shattering of their trust and the lives they thought they had, most straight spouses feel overcome with grief. As the shock wears off, our emotions can be overwhelming. Anger and rage at the how our husbands came out can skew our perceptions of what actually happened. Fear and loathing can make us sick or lead us to self-destructive behavior. Grief can easily lead to despair.

I was lucky to be able to fuel my actions in a relatively positive direction. I had access to the Internet, family, friends, support groups and information that could help me recover from the devastation of the betrayal and loss. Many women who live in rural communities or cultures that do not support a free exchange of information may not be as fortunate.

For many women, money becomes the barrier to a successful recovery. The fear of losing money in a divorce or losing the ability to make a living for herself and her kids will keep many women from accessing the help they need after their husband's disclosures. Lawyers cost money… therapists cost money… kids cost money. I get that. A portion of the proceeds of this book will provide access to legal counsel for women like us.

After years of struggling through many stages toward recovery, I decided to write the book I was looking for when the world split open. This is an attempt to offer others the help I tried so hard to find during my struggle for sanity. I offer my experiences and the experiences of other women who have walked similar paths to mine. As I talked with more and more women, it became apparent that each of our experiences varied widely, yet many similarities existed.

This book is not an editorial conglomeration of gay-straight marriages. This is a personal book written by and for the straight wife. It is a roadmap of discovery, divorce and ultimately, acceptance, as told through real life stories of three women who dealt with the discovery of their husbands' homosexuality in completely different ways.

*You're What?!* is about what we as women and mothers did to cope with an unexpected secret that shut us in an unfamiliar, secluded world. It is about how we walked our own paths, reengineered our lives and about the lessons we learned along the way. It is a survival guide for straight spouses. I hope this book will help you or your friend, sister or daughter who is married to a gay man get through the pain and anger and disillusionment and arrive at a place of wholeness that exemplifies forgiveness, growth, healing, hope and laughter.

My goal with this book is to help you believe that there is life after the death of your marriage to a gay man. You must understand first and foremost that you are not responsible for your husband's homosexuality. Your husband was born gay. It was in his DNA. You had no influence on this. This was not your husband's choice either, because homosexuality is not a choice. In most cases, your husband married you hoping that his sexuality would change, but it can't.

Through my own experiences and those of a number of other women, I hope to provide guidance and foresight into practical, sensible ways of protecting yourself, your children, your heart, your self-esteem and your money from the devastating effects that can occur after discovery of a change in sexual orientation of a life partner.

# 1 THE REVELATION

## Jackie, Mary, Carol

**Jackie** sat in the darkness of her basement at 2:30 in the morning searching for what she was terrified to find. At 2:45 a.m. she found it and threw up all over her desk. There he was, her husband of 19 years, on male internet dating sites looking for love. It's not like there wasn't any love at home. In fact, friends and family and casual acquaintances often called them a beautiful – no, gorgeous, loving – family. But there he was: *FLJockman1965*. The father of her children. She threw up again.

**Mary**, a physical therapist by trade, was on a camping trip with her husband and two kids in 2003. Her eldest, a 10-year-old son, was looking for his baseball glove in the tent. Dad had told him it was in the bag next to his backpack. As he rummaged through the tent, the boy found a small cooler that looked like his lunch box tucked inside Dad's duffle bag. He told his mother about the bottles of medicine he saw inside. Mary found out that her husband Jeff was gay by tracing the medication her son accidentally found to a medical clinic that supported HIV-infected patients.

**Carol** became suspicious that her husband was having an affair after 40 years of marriage when magazines for racy men's clothing started showing up in her mailbox. She grew more and more discomforted as the magazines multiplied. Eventually she noticed that the magazines never referenced females. She asked her husband if there was any reason to be concerned. He told her she was crazy and that he never ordered the magazines. Their love life slowly dwindled until Carol became withdrawn and desperate. Her husband Greg would eventually tell her that he was gay – but only after she had spent years trying to "fix" their love life.

## Jackie

Many hours before Jackie got sick to her stomach at the sight of her husband on her computer, Jackie's father, the most honorable, respected person in her life, called her on the phone to take her to lunch. Her dad never took her to lunch. Jackie was sure that either he had prostate cancer again or her mom was heading back for radiation for another lump in her breast. So convinced was she of impending doom that she called her siblings to inquire if they knew what was going on. Both her sisters and her brother were unnaturally quiet.

She arrived at the restaurant with a knot in the pit of her stomach. She couldn't connect her gut feeling to what was wrong. The hairs on the back of her neck weren't standing up, but she did feel as though something was not quite right. It was October in Wisconsin, a time of year when the leaves are gold and beautiful, but the wind is brutal. The lovely trees provided welcoming access to the typical side-of-the-highway restaurant, but the cold air that rushed in through the front door stung like an angry hornet. The Midwest fall chilled her bones. The humidity of fresh-cooked pasta and the scent of garlic and onions permeated the air, calming the nerves.

As her father wandered into the joint, Jackie's concern lightened a bit. Her dad wore a light golfing jacket and the same silly hat that she had seen him wear for 15 years. Although he didn't skip into the restaurant, he didn't drag himself in either. From his gait and the warm hug he gave her, Jackie concluded that it must be her mom they were there to discuss. Her dad wore a concerned look that reflected "I have something difficult to tell you" but not something as serious as "I'm going to die."

As Barry Manilow droned on over the speakers, Dad and his daughter shared 20 minutes of benign conversation before they ventured towards the elephant in the room.

"Who is sick – you or Mom?" Jackie asked. When her dad said "neither," she sighed with relief. The gentle, thoughtful man took a bite of his lasagna. "Too much garlic" was all he could say about this cuisine. Typically she would try to up his ante with a comment like, "Mine is so laden with garlic that there will be no evil spirits visiting me tonight!" But today was different and she just couldn't muster the courage to play their usual games.

Unable to handle the suspense any longer, Jackie asked, "Well then Dad, why are we meeting to eat pasta that could scare off a vampire on a Monday afternoon?"

What he was about to say would start the wheels of Jackie's life turning down a path she never chose to walk.

Grateful for her introduction, he wasted no more time. "I am finally willing to risk our loving relationship to tell you something," her father muttered as he pushed aside his plate. Every muscle in her petite body was strung as tight as a drum, waiting for the news of his impending death. She was prepared for sickness; she was primed for bad news. She was not at all prepared to hear that her husband was…GAY.

Her Dad led her into the information as gently as he could. In between a bite of limp noodles and a sip of coffee, her father, who is know for his compassion and generosity, quietly expressed his belief that Roger had been cheating on her. He told her the family news: her mother, brother and sisters had suspected for a long time that something was amiss in her marriage. Jackie's family had been watching and documenting her husband's actions for about three years. During this time, they were sure that he was having relations outside of her marriage. And they were almost sure he was not involved with another woman.

As her face grew ashen and her hands began to shake, her father reached across the table to put his loving hand on her shoulder. Throughout her childhood, this gesture had made her feel cared for, warm and loved. But today, at this moment, the feeling of his hand on her shoulder made Jackie wince in pain and bewilderment. She was not at all prepared to hear what was just said. She was not at all prepared to understand the depth of the love coming to her in the form of truth and honesty from her family. This lunch was becoming horrendously threatening.

Little did Jackie know that this would also be one of the most loving moments of her life.

Jackie tried to decide if she should ask questions about this revelation her family brought forth. Part of her didn't want to know any more. She wanted to rewind time and start this meeting over again. A sick parent she could deal with; it would be a heck of a lot better than her husband being gay! If she stood up now and walked away from the table, then perhaps this moment never existed. If she waited long enough, maybe her Dad would get up and say "April Fools Day!"

But this was October 10, 2005. Today was almost exactly 19 years since she wed the man of her dreams. She wanted to go back to the place she was all those years before, when she married Roger in a gorgeous ceremony. The yearning to return to that beautiful time overtook her senses.

Jackie is a romantic through and through. She judges movies on their "cry factor" and never forgets an anniversary or a birthday of those she loves. She took refuge from this conversation to dream of the vacations she took with Roger...to remember all the wonderful jewelry he had given her through the years and all the mushy cards he had written. She looked at her wedding ring and sobbed. While sitting across from her dad at the restaurant, a chunk of time was lost in a flood of loving memories of Roger.

When the memory bubble broke and she returned to her father, Jackie realized that she could not escape the vile words he had muttered. Against every sensation in her body, she asked, "Okay Dad, where did all of this come from?" Over the next half hour her father laid out the details of a highly complicated, well-executed investigation that had been taking place in the bowels of her family.

## Mary

It was a bright, sunny day in Northern California when Mary and Jeff and their two sons left for a long-awaited camping trip. Mary had been looking forward to this outing for months. She longed for some quiet days off, a break from the chaotic existence she led on a day-to-day basis. She wanted to get away from the reality of her life to connect with the man whom she loved and had grown slowly away from. She longed for his touch and his attention.

She ached for a few days without grocery shopping and filling the dishwasher and folding laundry and making beds and cooking dinner and brushing teeth and balancing the checkbook and helping with homework and attending conferences and vacuuming carpets and singing goodnight songs and making beds and giving baths and mowing the lawn and lining up dentist appointments and keeping peace with the neighbors and attending Boy Scouts and sitting through swimming class and then dutifully getting ready for bed in a negligee that implied she wanted to please her husband. Mary was the typical mother. She performed her daily duties and still made her man believe she wanted to have sex. In my opinion, she was a saint.

In reality, Mary had grown weary of the constant child care and family duties that had, over the last couple of years, become increasingly her responsibility. Then she blamed herself for Jeff's lack of enthusiasm in their sex life. Typical mother. Typical female.

Mary had planned the camping trip and packed the duffle bags and made all the arrangements for their journey. Usually Jeff enjoyed helping her plan family activities, but Mary had recently taken over these tasks, too. Jeff had been working extended hours during the week and had even begun going to the office on weekends. Mary had planned this getaway to give Jeff some release from his increasingly hectic work schedule. She was happy and content as she and Jeff and her two boys took off into the wilderness for a couple of days off.

Mary's relaxation lasted two and a half hours (that's how long it took to drive to the campground). Typical.

Jeff unloaded the bags from the back of the van and the family put up the tents. Then the luggage was unpacked and Martin was sent into the tent to find his baseball glove. He found the glove, and also found a hidden stash of items left in a cooler in the bottom of Dad's suitcase.

When little Martin told his mother of the medicines in Daddy's camping bag, she became suspicious. Jeff hadn't mentioned taking any medications. A few months earlier Mary had found a prescription of Viagra in the shaving kit Jeff packed for work trips, but after he had told her the reason for the prescription (to better service her sexual needs), she didn't give it a second thought. Now she started to think about it! Maybe Jeff had brought along the Viagra. Bless him.

However, she thought, why would there be more than one bottle of pills? There was no real reason to suspect that Jeff was under the influence of drugs. Or was there? Mary had spent the last 10 years proudly announcing to her church groups that neither she nor her husband ever took recreational drugs. No Ritalin.

No sleeping pills. No downers, no uppers, no marijuana, nothing.

Panic didn't get the best of her during the camping trip, but it sure did sneak into her life upon returning home. Jeff went to bed early that night, of course, because he was "tired." He went to sleep and she went to work looking for drugs. There were no new bottles in the medicine chest in their bedroom. There were no bottles hidden under the bed. There were no pills in his office or his sock drawer or his private drawer where he hid sex toys that Mary had never seen before.

When her son Martin told Mary about the drugs he found in the tent, Mary did what most caring moms would do. She told her son not to worry. The bottles probably were full of vitamins.

Mary called her doctor to request information about any new prescriptions. No new prescriptions had been written since her son needed amoxicillin for his earache the year before. She then called her pharmacy to see if medications were due to be picked up. Nothing. Shit.

A day full of anticipation and anger went by. Mary sifted through numerous fits of anxiety. She started to think about the other details in their lives that he had been omitting. Where the hell was he working all these late hours? She kept trying to call him at the office but his phone would go straight to voicemail. And when he worked on weekends, his cell phone would also go to voicemail. There was a feeling in Mary's gut that the trail of the medicines in Jeff's luggage would lead to many unanswered questions.

After her husband had gone to sleep the next evening, Mary searched his car. She found a small cooler jammed under his seat that contained three bottles of medicine. She swiftly wrote down the names and the dosages of the drugs and returned the container to its original location. The next morning, after the kids had gone off to school, Mary called a local free medical clinic to inquire about Retrovir. She was told by the answer line attendant that Retrovir is a nucleoside analog reverse transcriptase inhibitor. Panicked, she asked the agent to put that in plain English. "Retrovir," she was told, "is Zidovudine, also known as AZT. It is used to treat HIV infection."

Mary's last memory of that afternoon was dropping the phone and passing out on the kitchen floor.

## Carol

In the summer, Carol and Greg usually spent their Sunday afternoons sitting on the porch looking over the cornfields. In winter they sat near the fireplace reading a book or completing the New York Times crossword puzzle. They loved just being together, each working on his or her projects, drinking lemonade and talking about the previous week's activities. They had spent most Sundays in this fashion for almost four decades.

Carol and Greg had a good life. Although they had no children of their own, Greg's many brothers and sisters had provided them with numerous nieces and nephews who frequently frolicked on the farm. Both Carol and Greg were active in their rural farming town in western Nebraska. They worked hard, attended church on Sunday mornings and volunteered often at the community center.

Carol met Greg in high school. She was a shy, sweet gal whose dad owned the town hardware store. She longed for a life outside of Nebraska but she was happy to put those dreams on hold when she met her future husband. Greg was the oldest son of a hard working, hard drinking, God-fearing farmer whose land had been tilled by the last three generations of his family. Greg would follow in the footsteps of the first-born sons in all the generations before him. He would stay on the prairie and raise a family and live off the land.

Carol fell in love with Greg in their senior year. He was a kind, gentle soul who treated her like a princess and promised her a good life. They were married in the town chapel five months after graduation.

As the years progressed, Greg's anger about not conceiving children with Carol lessened and the couple fell into a groove of enjoying a quiet life on the farm. When Greg was 58-years-old his father passed away. Carol thought her husband would be miserable. In fact, the passing of his father left Greg with a sense of freedom she had never witnessed before. Suddenly Greg wanted to take trips with her to places like Southern Florida and San Francisco. He ordered internet service for their home and inquired about putting a satellite TV dish on the roof. Greg had never mentioned wanting satellite TV before. His father said the devil enters a home through the television, so neither Greg nor his brothers and sisters had ever had televisions. At least they never admitted it.

As the months passed, Greg spent more and more time alone in his study on the internet instead of rocking with Carol on the porch. A few years passed before she realized that she was always alone in their home. Greg's desire to help make dinner or share their crossword puzzle had been replaced by his desire to read his magazines alone in his study.

Slowly, signs of her husband's changing sexual orientation started showing up. Catalogues of men's racy undergarments were delivered to their mailbox. Subscriptions to magazines like *Men's Fitness* and *The Advocate* showed up on her credit card statement.

They went from having a "normal" sex life to never having sex. When Carol grew despondent over the loss of intimacy with her husband, she went to her church to ask for guidance. She was told by her minister to pay more attention to her husband. She was told to fix him better meals, freshen up her appearance and make more of an effort to please him in bed.

Carol gave it everything she had for the following six months. She cooked all of Greg's favorite meals. She bought new clothes and wore pretty lipsticks and mascara. She kept a clean, bright home. She wore negligees to bed and begged to please her man. What she received in return was rejection, solitude and a badly bruised ego. The harder she tried to take care of Greg's needs, the more he pushed her away and moved into isolation.

When she could no longer take the rejection, she approached her husband and asked him what was happening. Together they cried as Greg revealed that he loved Carol but that he had recently "become" a gay man. He talked about how his life changed after the death of his father and about how he began dreaming of having sex with men. He told her of how he had left her for the day in San Francisco when she was shopping to have sex with men in the gay community. He wanted to see if he was "really gay" or if he was just confused. He told her of how much he wanted to hate the sex with men in San Francisco, but how "right" it felt. He had sex with five different men over the span of their six day vacation. He also had sex with her. Carol did not grasp the gravity of Greg's statement, or the physical danger he had put her in during that trip. It would take her years of therapy to understand how selfish Greg's actions were. How could he have had sex with other men, then come home to her and have sex with her? How could this man, whom she had loved for 40 years, so blatantly disregard her health and happiness? How could he have been so disgusting?

Greg tried to lessen the blow by telling Carol that he did not have a lover, and was not having consistent sex outside of their marriage. He was so sorry he'd hurt Carol. He just couldn't bring himself to tell her. He was waiting for his feelings to change. He didn't want to be gay and he didn't want anyone else to know.

"Please don't tell anyone about this," he begged.

With those few words he opened the door to the proverbial "closet" and locked Carol in with him. For the next hour Greg cried to Carol about how he wanted to stay married to her, but he wanted to have sex with men sometimes. Could they just try to work something out?

# 2 HAPPY MARRIAGES

## *Jackie*

Nineteen years before this discussion with her father, Jackie's dream of marrying the perfect man came true. The creative, strong, smart, athletic, fun gal who had lived all over the world married the handsome, intelligent man who made her feel like a princess. Although Roger had tendencies to be less of a "guy's guy" than other man she had dated, he also was more loved by her girlfriends than any other suitor. Roger was not one to spend Sunday afternoons watching football and guzzling beer with the boys. He was the guy who opened doors for women, told them they were beautiful and treated them with respect.

Back then Jackie and Roger filled the holes in each other's lives. He was organized. She was random. He transformed a rundown home into a beauty. She showed him how to relax. He did impeccable laundry and strove to be a master chef. She set off all the fire alarms in the house with her cooking. He was structured, uptight and Republican. She was relaxed, athletic and committed to freethinking. They completed each other.

Roger was raised in a Catholic family. Jackie was raised in a family where religion was a floating concept. She was raised with strong values of morality and ethics, but no definitive religion.

Little did Jackie know at the time that the religious undertones of Roger's family would be one of the strongest factors keeping his "secret" life under wraps. Prior to their engagement, Roger and Jackie discussed the doctrine that infiltrated his family. They also discussed Jackie's desire to live free of religious domination. To her, Catholicism represented the repression of the female. Whether it was intentional or not, she was brought up believing that the Catholic religion gave little choice to women who "truly" believed. From Young Life in high school, her life was surrounded by messages of Catholicism being "anti-choice" and not "pro-women." It was a religion that just kept showing up in her life – that permeated her being without invitation.

Roger was raised in a family of strong women. His mom, Maggie, was one of Jackie's favorite feminists of all time. She was married to Roger's father Patrick for 40 years. Patrick was an overwhelming man whose great big personality often flattened the ideas of his family like a steamroller. He and Maggie, a stay-at-home mom who raised great kids and sheltered them from many of the difficulties that come from an overwhelming father, brought the kids to church every Sunday. Maggie was a true, dyed-in-the-wool Catholic. A huge influence in her son's life, Maggie died a few years before Roger "turned gay." She was a lovely woman who taught her children to respect their parents, be polite and, above all, to respect the church.

Jackie was also brought up in a family of strong women. Her mom, a nurse by trade, was the only student in her high school class to earn an academic scholarship. She'd set her sights on getting out of her small rural town to continue her education after high school. With no money in the family to enroll in classes, Jackie's role model set her sights on the only financial award available to her…and got it.

When Jackie was courting Maggie's son, she was young, full of confidence and ready to take on the world. Any religion that restricted a woman's right to make choices about her body and her family planning was insane to her. At the age of 28 she was sure of one thing – she was NOT ready to have kids. The Catholic Church would not own her. She was an intelligent, sassy woman who loved her man, but wanted freedom to choose how their lives would proceed. She would never be married in a Catholic church.

It was always assumed that the children of Maggie's family would be married as Catholics, to Catholics. Unfortunately, however, life didn't exactly work out that way. Roger's sister and brother married Lutherans. Jackie was sure that the family's paths to Satan were laid in concrete after she chose a non-catholic chaplain to marry her and Roger. Chaplain Don had a license to preside over a variety of religious ceremonies. He was a man of the world who had worked his ministry with all kinds of people who had varying ideas of what a relationship with God looked like. She loved him. He met with the couple, provided his blessing and they were on their way.

Little did Jackie know at the time that she was setting a precedent for tolerance in her home and in her relationships. The simple act of hiring a non-traditional clergyperson showed her fiancé that she could tolerate a liberal life that was outside the boundaries of the "normal" lives of her friends. With her actions, Jackie was showing her groom the openness of her soul…and who she would be nineteen years later when he succumbed to becoming the gay man who lived just below the surface.

## Mary

For the first six years of their marriage, Mary and Jeff were the kind of couple that others loved to be around. They were outgoing and lighthearted and fun. They were loud and crazy and impulsive. They drove beautiful cars, kept their bodies in perfect shape at the finest health clubs, took great vacations and attended church regularly. They were married in the Presbyterian church down the street and they led couples bible studies on Wednesday nights.

Jeff was a traveling salesman in those years, on the road for a few days every other week. Mary was thrilled to give birth to their son shortly after they were married. Then another child arrived. Mary and Jeff continued a healthy social life even after the children were born. They were members of numerous social circles and were dedicated to a helping other couples cope with life through a relationship with Christ.

As their reputation for leading wonderful couples group sessions grew, Mary and Jeff became more and more comfortable in sharing their own stories with others. They told newly married couples about their romances. New parents learned about their partnership in raising children. More mature couples were told about Jeff and Mary's dedication to building a life together of honesty and integrity. They won everyone over with their sincerity.

## Carol

Carol was just 19-years-old when she married Greg. They were Nebraska high school sweethearts who had fallen in love the year before they got married. Neither Greg nor Carol had ever had a serious relationship with anyone else. Their romance blossomed at a church group, where the "good kids" gathered to worship and spread the good news about religious faith. As other kids attended football games and loitered at McDonalds, both Greg and Carol were encouraged by their families to attend worship services regularly and curtail social engagements with the opposite sex to church-sponsored activities.

Greg's parents loved Carol from the day they met her. She was from a prominent family that was well-known in the community. Her parents were important members of the local Baptist church. She was present at all the significant spiritual events in her city. Greg's parents courted both Carol and her family to ensure a proper connection for their son, who was sheltered by a strong religious family.

Greg loved Carol and married her. For many years they led a typical rural life full of baseball and potluck suppers and card nights with the neighbors. Greg was verbal about his desire for children. Everyone in the town knew he wanted six kids – just like his parents had. Both Carol and Greg were disappointed by their inability to procreate; however, they loved being good aunts and uncles.

As the years passed, people in the community started commenting about the gradual disappearance of Carol and Greg. The couple was seen with less and less frequency at religious events. Carol no longer attended all the neighborhood get-togethers. She was no longer a fixture at book club. They were no longer active in church group events.

Her friends knew that Carol's life with Greg was changing. Keeping up the increasingly perfect house that Greg demanded exhausted her. He seemed to love her, but he became a difficult husband. He retreated from the social life that had kept the couple connected to the community.

He had developed a need for order and cleanliness that left Carol with little time to breathe. The couple no longer attended Wednesday evening chapel events because Greg insisted on mowing and tilling and raking the lawn on Wednesday nights. Every evening had been dedicated to a task from ironing sheets to cleaning floors to organizing the garage. Greg had become so obsessive about organization that there was no longer time in their lives for social gatherings. Carol had slowly become a prisoner in a home that Greg was ruling. It would be years before Carol understood that Greg's compulsive behavior and avoidance of religious events was partly his attempt to control the latent feelings of homosexuality that were infiltrating his being.

Another way Greg tried to control his surroundings to hide his true feelings was restricting information. He strictly forbade Carol from having a TV in the home, and mandated certain radio channels. He allowed her to only read materials that he chose. He eventually became so obsessive that he even forbade the church from sending any written materials to their home. Greg shut Carol inside a prison of his creation.

Eventually their nieces and nephews stopped coming by to play. As neighbors watched, Greg slowly retreated from his environment by developing rules and order that created a wall around him and Carol. He formed a shield of well-defined actions that dictated how his family would function. He thought this wall of order and "rightness" would keep him safe from the demons that lurked just below the surface of his consciousness.

# Discussion:
*Do religious and social influences lead gay men to marry straight women?*

All of these women's stories have something in common. There is an underlying thread of social, religious and personal expectations that lead gay men to marry straight women. These same influences then keep them from acknowledging the truth about their own sexuality.

Most gay men marry to conform to the expectations of family or society. They also marry because they want the same things as we (straight women) want – children and the long-term companionship of a family with children. Some gay men marry specifically to father children. They follow the religious and social guidelines that say one must be married before having kids. They want kids…so they marry.

It is my belief, however, that most gay men who marry women love their wives when the marry them. Sincere affection and true love is common for gay/straight couples both before and after disclosure of a man's homosexuality. Jackie, Mary and Carol claim, as I do, that true love was mutual at the moment of matrimony.

There are other needs that a wife fulfills for a gay husband, aside from care-giving or bearing children. Traditional wives can be great friends and partners. We can support and even enhance a man's career. We can provide a second income, a comfortable home and a great social life.

In her book "Straight Wives: Shattered Lives," Bonnie Kaye, M.Ed., states that men do not get married to destroy the lives of their spouses, but rather to save theirs. I agree. Some studies show that gay men who marry straight women hope that if they love you hard enough, they will not, in fact, be gay.

They hope that if they can have good enough sex with you, then they just may be straight.

So they continue to live their typical married life with kids. And then along comes the male menopause, or whatever you care to call it. The trigger could be a period of high stress, such as the threat of redundancy at work, difficulties with the marriage or financial loss. Often, it happens by the time the children have grown up and are about to leave the nest. The gay husband wakes up to the fact that he has not fulfilled his true sexuality. Yes, he is still gay, he realizes. He may start to look around at other men (if he has not always done this, subconsciously). He may start to play around a bit - go to the local gay sauna, visit the odd gay bar or club, venture onto the internet seeking pictures and friends. The last thing he will do before starting this is to talk to his wife.

Before long, the gay husband may have gay partners with whom he meets for casual sex. He may even fall in love with one particular guy, sometimes much younger than himself. All of the time, he may be putting himself and his wife at risk of sexually transmitted diseases including HIV, hepatitis, syphilis and so on. If he has any conscience at this time (and any responsibility) he may well start to visit the local GUM Clinic where he can undertake tests anonymously. He is relieved to discover that the tests prove negative. Then he thinks about telling his wife.

He talks to his friends in the gay community. He pulls away from his straight friends. He is told by most of his "new" community to hide his activities from his wife. They tell him that in divorce he will lose his kids and lose his money. He will lose his house and his friends. He will lose everything. Typically at this point, a gay man in a marriage will decide to continue deceiving his wife until he is "sure" that he is gay.

The difficulties of a man coming to terms with

his homosexuality within a marriage is an issue that the media has covered in great detail – usually to the benefit of the gay spouse. On a recent episode of Oprah, former New Jersey Governor Jim McGreevey talked about how "the closet starves a man and when he gets a chance, he gorges 'til it sickens him." He discussed the fact that the only place he could discover "who he was" was in places of anonymity, in dark shadows where he could experiment sexually. Jim talked about the private and agonizing story behind his very public fall from office. You could almost hear a sigh of sorrow for Mr. McGreevey after he was done recounting his tale of coming out. Even I felt sorry for him.

Then I started thinking about his wife. Where was she in this discussion? Where were the cries of sympathy for a woman whose husband lied to her, cheated on her and possibly exposed her to grave physical harm in the form of HIV/AIDS or venereal diseases? For wives whose husbands had secret liaisons before coming out, the disclosure of homosexuality presents a life-or-death dilemma. We get tested for STDs and AIDS and wait anxiously for results. Women like Dina McGreevy (Jim's ex-wife) can't understand why their husbands, who claim to love them dearly, put them at risk for a fatal disease and put their children at risk of losing both parents. Oprah's show did a nice job of highlighting the straight wife's lonely existence; however, as usual, the show centered on the much sexier topic of the husband's departure from "the closet."

Here's the problem: our husbands struggle with their homosexuality for years. They deny who they are because THEY DON'T WANT TO BE GAY. They spend decades denying their sexual confusion to themselves and others. They see themselves as devoted husbands, conscientious fathers and suburban homeowners. Many of these men live very productive, loving lives with their wives and children prior to their coming out. What typically brings them to the point of crisis in their 40s, 50s and 60s is their first emotional connection with another man, or a "trigger" like the death of his parents or the realization that he hates his job. For gay men in heterosexual marriages, even after they can no longer live the status quo, the pull of a "typical" married life with children remains powerful. Many of these men are desperate to preserve their marriages and to continue receiving the emotional and financial grounding of wives and children.

I acknowledge and sympathize with their internal struggle, but I think it is time for the straight spouse to have her time in the media. Men who are gay and married to a woman without her knowledge of his orientation are hiding behind the security of a wife and a family, leading the "straight" life. They desire men sexually, and often have sexual encounters with other men while their loving wives continue taking care of their home and their children. The wife suffers in silence from sexual-emotional abuse, making her feel as though she is the "abnormal" one, or that she is playing a role in the deterioration of the sexual bond with her spouse. The sexual rejection by the majority of gay men strips away the sexual esteem of women. Due to a lack of any sexual activity, we can feel undesirable or that we have extreme sexual needs. The gay man in these relationships is not the only one who suffers with sexual issues – the straight wife also carries a burden.

My word of advice to any woman married to or in a committed relationship with a gay man is this: remember that when your husband is gay or bisexual, the one person who you should not blame is yourself. The "if only's" don't apply here. "If only I had made myself more attractive to him," would work if he was going after women. But if he is homosexual, there is little that you could do to stop it. Please believe that your husband began this marriage because he loved you when he married you. You were exactly what he wanted. And up until he started acting on his homosexual feelings, you and the kids were exactly what he lived for.

If he is gay, he is probably still married because the social and religious pressures he is feeling are too overwhelming for him. Although deceiving you is not acceptable (in fact, it is horrible), he may be doing so only because he is truly unable to face the realities of what will happen to him if he is honest. There is nothing you could have done to change him. He is gay – and it has nothing to do with you.

So don't ever blame yourself!

# 3 DISCOVERY

## *Jackie*

Three days prior to Jackie's luncheon at Olive Garden with her dad, Roger made the one mistake that all prosecuting attorneys look for. He made the mistake that proved him guilty beyond a shadow of a doubt. He made the mistake that allowed her family to finally risk telling her that Roger was gay. You see, on that fateful day in October, 2005, Roger missed Jackie's father's 65th birthday party. He was on a vacation with "the guys."

Jackie's family had planned a special celebration for her father's birthday. One sister came in from Tacoma, the other from San Diego, and her brother and his family came in from Utah. One week prior to the event, Roger informed Jackie that he would miss this celebration due to a last minute opportunity with the guys. He said he was going to Montréal for a special get-together with friends. He would be gone five days. When her father inquired about Roger's absence at the event, Jackie, in her typically naïve fashion, mentioned that her husband was in Montréal with friends. That was the last they spoke of Roger's absence for the evening.

Roger had told Jackie the location of this trip. This particular piece of information would ultimately be his downfall.

It took no time at all for her brother, Larry, to start salivating. The morning after the party he jumped into action. Before the rest of the family had risen from their beds, Larry had already spent an hour on the internet researching what special events were occurring in Montréal over the weekend. What Jackie's brother found was be the linchpin of Roger's double life.

Eventually, every gay man who is living a gay life while hiding in the security of a marriage will make errors. These mistakes will tip you off to his activities. If you are the wife of a gay man and you are unaware of your husband's orientation, it is very likely that you will not be the one to identify your husband's sexual identity. Others will do it for you. Keep your eyes and ears open to places your husband may be going, and take note of any unusual destinations that he may travel to. Jackie found out about Roger's gay sexual activities because he missed her father's birthday party.

On that weekend in October, the BBCM Foundation (which stands for Bad Boy Club Montreal) held one of the leading events of the gay circuit and of the international music scene. The event is called the Black and Blue Festival. It is the biggest event of its kind in North America, and is widely recognized as "one of the best parties on the planet." Participants and observers from all over the world claim it is one of the most spectacular events ever produced.

Jackie's father encouraged her to get online and research the Black and Blue Festival. He begged her to Google some of the cities Roger had attended recently and the municipal websites of those locations over the dates of his absences. Her dad begged her to get on the 'net and get smart about her husband's life!

Jackie was devastated about what she had just heard and she reacted violently. "Dad," she said, "I can't believe you are trying so hard to destroy Roger! I know that you and Mom are suspicious of him, but you have always been kind and accepting. Why now, after nineteen years of marriage, would you try to destroy what we have?" She was so angry and disappointed she couldn't think straight.

Jackie stood up from her chair, crying, and told her father that he was wrong. "If Roger was gay I would have known it by now! Roger loves me, Roger has always loved me and Roger would never do this to me. You and Mom and everyone else are just wrong!" Jackie stood up with the conviction of a bullfighter and started to walk away from the table. It was then that her Dad did something she will never forget. This gentle, kind man who had never raised his voice, pleaded for her to take some time to consider what had been presented.

He put a one-hundred dollar bill in her hand and said, "Take this and hire a computer geek to help you find out about what Roger's been doing." She had no idea what he meant, but she took the money anyway. She put the money in her pocket and kissed her father on the cheek. By now she was crying so hard that her words of "I love you, Dad" were mumbled through the tears running down her face.

As Jackie sat down behind the wheel of her car, her emotions overwhelmed her. She sat in that parking lot for ten minutes with thoughts of Roger's actions swirling through her mind: I would know, damn it, I would know if he's gay… for God's sake, we've been married for so long!

Jackie has no idea how she got home that day. She is convinced that car must have driven itself, for she has no memory of turning the key, merging onto the exit ramp, or stopping to pick up the mail that was in her hand as she reached to turn off the ignition.

## Mary

When Mary awoke, she wondered how long she had been lying there on the hardwood floor. The last thing she remembered was hearing the pharmacist on the other end of the telephone line say "these medicines are used to treat HIV/AIDS." She did not remember dropping the phone or passing out. Thankfully it was still only 11:30 a.m. so she had plenty of time to get her act together before her son returned from school.

Mary remembers going upstairs to take a shower. She remembers looking in the medicine cabinet and crying. She distinctly remembers considering suicide. While the warm shower water fell over her body, Mary thought for a moment about using her razor to cut her wrists. She was distraught. What does it mean that Jeff has HIV? Does she have it? How long has he had this disease? Why didn't he tell her? Will she survive being a single parent? Will she live to be a single parent? The questions were overwhelming.

Finally the warm water ran cold and she was forced to leave the shower. Thank God she did not take her life.

Mary put on her favorite jeans and a t-shirt. And she cried all afternoon. She climbed into bed, sobbed until her chest hurt and fell asleep exhausted.

## Carol

As Carol watched her husband grow distant, she experienced many of the same emotions any wife feels as her husband retreats from her. She grew more and more despondent by the day. She blamed herself for Greg's loss of interest in their sex life. Her desire to reestablish his sexual interest drove her to self-destructive activities. Carol started hiding alcohol in her washroom. She became neurotic in her quest for order and cleanliness in the home. She fixed elaborate meals for her husband and then ran to the bathroom to throw up the food she ate. She took pills to go to sleep and others to stay awake. She became reluctant to visit friends. She avoided shopping, which she used to love, for fear of running into acquaintances who may ask her personal questions. She lost her dedication to her church and she questioned her faith.

When Greg revealed his homosexuality, Carol actually was overcome with a sense of relief for a short period. Finally she understood that there was nothing she could do to change him. She could stop binging and purging. She could start eating normally again. She could relax. She could stop drinking. She could stop taking pills.

Or could she?

## Discussion:
*How do the discoveries of infidelity and homosexuality affect the straight spouse?*

When finding out about our husbands' homosexuality, most of us either explode in anger or are paralyzed by disbelief. Receiving the unexpected news that your husband is gay is a truly shocking experience. Some women's feelings are like a car wreck. They are dazed and confused. This is exactly what happened to me, Jackie, Carol and Mary. In Jackie's case, the car drove itself home and she was in it. She was so dazed that she can't remember getting home. This is typical. Shock and disbelief are the most common first reactions.

Often, however, illness follows the shock. For

weeks following the discussion with her dad, Jackie went through a series of physical ailments. A lack of sleep left her vulnerable to sore throats, colds and even hair loss. In the books "My Husband is Gay" and "Straight Wives: Shattered Lives," one woman after another recounts suffering from symptoms as simple as colds to those as extreme as heart attacks after the coming out of her spouse. Anxiety is the most common ailment, and we all know what kind of destruction anxiety can wreak on the human body.

Can it be proven that there is a direct cause-effect relationship between the "coming out" of a spouse and physical ailments of the other? Maybe not, but the link between serious distress and physical problems is real.

The immediate sense of betrayal can be unbearable for women like Mary, who had no prior suspicion of her husbands' sexual orientation. The initial shock can quickly change to hurt. Many women eventually are drawn to self-destructive behavior due to the pain of betrayal and loss. We may turn to alcohol or drugs or violence to escape the pain.

Whether spouses divorce at once or try to make the marriage work, it may take months or even years to fully realize the profound impact that the partner's coming out has had. Those who divorce (like all of us in this book) become preoccupied with the separation problems and the endless details of the divorce. Those who stay married are adapting to their husband's homosexual activities. In either case, our own identities are buried in the process of dealing with the coming out crisis.

For most spouses, the first clues of lost identity come some time in the year after the coming out. Whether they stay married or separate, straight spouses often find themselves exhausted from the cumulative effect of just getting through each day.

Add children to the mix and a woman's coping mechanisms can go from overdrive to a total shutdown. Many of us develop severe symptoms, including full-blown depression. We can be overcome by desolation, loneliness and fatigue.

If you have just found out about your husband's change in sexual orientation, please seek guidance. Don't keep the secret to yourself. Turn to a friend or therapist for help. Be aware that you are very vulnerable and that you may very well get sick if you keep this trapped inside. Of course, your first action should be to get a physical exam and an AIDS test (more on that in following chapters).

Self-nurturing is one of the best ways to overcome the desolation you may feel. Rest, a balanced diet, physical activity and relaxation with friends are powerful ways to get back your physical and emotional strength.

Non-thinking experiences like listening to music can also enhance the healing process. Music can release significant sorrowful emotions. I welcomed tears by playing sad country music songs in my car. I would cry like a baby by myself and I always felt better afterwards. When I felt more like screaming than crying, I would wait for the kids to get on the bus and then return to an empty house to scream and throw books at the walls. My favorite books to destroy in my anger and frustration were those we had collected about the Caribbean and Europe and all the other places we contemplated for retirement.

You may also find solace in daydreaming when things get bad. I think daydreaming was a comfortable way to escape my fears for a while. While walking the isles at the grocery store, I imagined sitting on top of a mountain peak breathing fresh crisp air under crystal blue skies. Then, while watching my son's baseball practice, I imagined playing in the sand at the ocean with the kids. In both emotional escapes, I dreamed my ex-husband was in a suit in a cubicle in a dark office tied to a desk with nothing but a phone and a computer. He was living the hell I banished him to. I encourage you to welcome all your tears and anger and daydreams. They will help you heal and (unless you act on your dreams) they won'l hurt anyone else.

Sleeplessness is a real problem for people in the midst of grief or crisis. I was like most women – waking up at 3:00 a.m. and staying awake for hours before falling asleep again right before my alarm rang. After weeks of such insomnia, I approached my doctor for assistance. The sleeping pills he prescribed helped me recover my physical well-being and allowed me to focus during the day. I was afraid to take the pills – afraid to get "addicted," however my doctor said the medicine was not addictive and would provide me with the rest I needed to get back to normal. He only gave me enough for six weeks. That was all I really needed.

If you have a health care advocate, don't hesitate to approach him/her for support. Most of all: be kind to yourself. Try to minimize the use of alcohol, drugs or cigarettes. They may get you through the day, but they won't help you heal. In addition, they carry the greater danger of dependence or addiction.

# 4 INTERNET SECRETS

After leaving her father, *Jackie* returned home to the typical loads of laundry and dirty dishes that had become a cornerstone of her life. She remembers, before she was married, how people regarded her as a "free spirit." When she met Roger she was an easy-going, relaxed, fun young gal who was smart, spirited and somewhat disorganized.

As she pulled into the driveway and pushed the button to open the garage door, she started to see the loss of the old Jackie in her life. The garage, like the rest of her home, was supremely organized. Every bike had its place, every tool was placed neatly in the toolboxes, every ski, skateboard, and scooter was hung perfectly in place. There was not even dirt on the garage floor, for this was not accepted in Roger's highly organized home.

In a way, she was grateful that Roger was returning home from Montréal that night. Because of his impending return, she purposefully filled the rest of the day with the tasks that needed to be accomplished in order to have harmony in her home. She washed, folded and put away laundry. She vacuumed, cleaned the kitchen and made sure that all beds were perfect. She even made a beautiful dinner so that the kids would have the opportunity to relax and hear about Roger's trip and to tell him about Papa's birthday celebration. She went into overdrive denying the occurrences of the day. She, like many women in her situation, was in a state of shock and denial.

Jackie rejected her father's prognosis, sure that he was wrong about Roger. She was confident that Roger's frequent trips with "the guys" were just like her trips with "the gals." She was sure that tonight, at dinner, the kids and she would hear about a trip filled with fishing, hunting, or some other male activity.

Roger came home that night as the kids and she were just finishing their chicken pot pie. As the kids told their dad stories of the family celebration, she watched Roger's face for any sign of guilt. He joined in their conversation with the ease of a figure skater gliding on ice. He regaled them with stories of the fun that he and his friends had had in Canada and, too, he told of a fundraiser they attended that had dancers from Cirque De Soleil. His response to her inquiry as to the benefactor of the fundraiser was "an organization that helps families." She could feel her blood begin to boil. Maybe, just maybe, her dad might be right. Maybe he was lying to her.

Roger put the kids to bed and apologized to Jackie for his sleepiness. Of course, the idea of a "welcome home" quickie was not even mentioned.

"I didn't get a lot of sleep on this trip, so I'm heading to bed early tonight. We'll talk some more tomorrow, okay?" Roger asked as though he had nothing to hide.

"Of course, honey," Jackie said in a typical fashion, "let's talk more tomorrow." Their sexual encounters with each other were so infrequent these days that Jackie was not surprised at Roger's lack of enthusiasm.

Jackie fell asleep with Roger that night, sure that feeling his closeness would make her fears go away. As she lay next to him in bed, she listened to his breathing get slower and slower. By 11:30 p.m. she was sure that he was asleep. She had never been the victim of insomnia; however, this night would hold no sleep for her. In the dark, she put on a big, fluffy robe and slippers, poured herself a Coke, and headed for the home office. She turned on the desk lamp and ignited the power switch on the computer. Terrified that Roger might awaken and ask her what she was doing, she made sure to have an open file from her bank account ready, so that she could frame her activities in the context of insomnia and checkbook balancing. Armed with the task of discovery, she Googled through web pages like a bull in a china shop.

For three hours, Jackie read everything she could. Her internet searches focused on subjects like: "gay," "gay man," "gay husbands," "homosexuality," "straight," "coming out," "AIDS," "HIV," "bisexual," "secret lives," "straight wives," "sexual orientation," "sexual identity," "gay festivals" and "coming out of the closet."

By 1:00 a.m. Jackie was sick of touchy-feely articles and she wanted some facts. She began a web search for male dating websites. A futile 30 minutes spent in this endeavor led her to dead ends. She was unfamiliar at this point in her life with the jargon of gay porn websites. Here she was, a 42-year-old white housewife using the tools of her marketing degree to research topics that she knew nothing about. It took her another 30 minutes to understand that the world she was investigating had a jargon all its own.

As soon as Jackie realized that the term "dating" in the world of homosexual men on the internet was "hooking up," she was able to also understand that genteel terminology like "pretty" and "good-looking" and "adventurous" that her girlfriends used on Match.com and E-Harmony were not relevant. Shortly, she realized that words such as "cute," "fun" and "sexy" were replaced on these male dating sites with words like "hot," "beefy" and "versatile."

As she searched her computer's hard drive, she found a file called "Temporary Internet Files." Jackie had no idea what she was doing, but she figured she had nothing to lose. Opening "Temporary Internet Files" was like opening a Pandora's box. Within a moment, her screen was flooded with websites that had been visited within the last month. She chose a website named something like Menformen.net as the first of many that she would visit over the next couple of days.

While researching Jackie's story I went to many sites like Menformen.net and here is what I saw: a display of nude and semi-nude photos of gay men. I also read raw comments about each man's sexual prowess and their desires to attract mostly anonymous sexual partners. In fairness I must say that porn websites exist on the internet for all sexual orientations, in all shapes and forms. Menformen.net and the others mentioned in this book are not representative of all gay dating sites. They are mentioned here only because these are sites that our straight wives researched when looking for their husbands who were not yet "out."

"Yes," Jackie said to herself, "Roger has visited these sites, but he's not on them." For an hour, she researched this site with the veracity of a dog looking for a buried bone. She studied the language that was used on this site. She studied the terminology that they used for describing themselves. Here are some "clean" highlights she noted on sexually explicit gay male websites:

## Question:
*Phrases used on Male Gay Sex websites:*

Do you have any venereal diseases?
*Are you clean?*

Do you have HIV or AIDS?
*Are you NEG or POS?*

Do you prefer multiple partners?
*Are you into 3-ways?*

I don't want a relationship.
*No drama, no future.*

Have you been circumcised?
*Are you cut or uncut?*

Do you want to use sexual aids?
*Toys? Leather?*

Are you in a relationship?
*Strings or no strings?*

Does size matter?
*Are you hung?*

Do you have a nice body?
*Are you cut or beefy?*

**You get the idea.**

As soon as Jackie understood the basics of these person-als websites, she decided to look for Roger. It did not take her long to discover that, just like buying jewelry on QVC. com, you had to be a member to find additional informa-tion. She quickly understood that she would need a user name for each website in order to track down her husband. It was at this point that she began to start feeling sick.

At 2:30 a.m., Jackie was exhausted. But she was also in-trigued and terrified. Fury and fear can do strange things to a woman. She became obsessed with finding out if Roger was on any of these websites. She was so emotionally de-pleted however, that this would have to wait for another day. For four hours she had been sitting in her home office in her pajamas, in the dark, praying that the kids would not wake up and that Roger would not stir.

She turned off the computer and headed back upstairs. At the threshold to her bedroom she started to cry her first tears of sorrow. Alone in the dark, she sobbed lightly, afraid to make a sound. She could hear Roger's breathing, rhyth-mic as usual, and she mourned a life that would never be. The sounds emanating from her bedroom- the room where they used to make love, discuss their dreams, watch Satur-day morning cartoons with the kids - were now the sounds of a cheater. The slow, deep breathing of her husband that used to give her comfort now gave her chills. She remem-bers standing above the bed, unmoving, for five minutes.

Jackie walked to each kid's room in the dark and listened to them sleep. She said a prayer for the kids and tucked them both into the safety and security of their familiar blankets. She left tears on their cheeks as she kissed them goodnight. What would happen to them and to her?

And then she almost threw up again. Damn it – she forgot to erase her actions on the computer! Roger always checked the family computer in the morning before heading to work. He would see a trail that would blow her cover. She ran back downstairs, booted up the machine, and erased all the temporary internet files that were left on the hard drive. She also erased the history file.

Months prior to this awful evening, Jackie's ten-year-old daughter had inadvertently taught her to erase the "history" file by expressing interest in her mom's online shopping habits.

"How do you know that I shop online?" Jackie asked.

Immediately she got the "you are a dummy" look before Kimberly replied, "Mom, duh, I know all the stores that you visit online. They are on the drop down history file."

"The what?"

"The history file that drops down when you start typing in the website you are looking for. It tells you what sights you visited that day, or that week or that month or since you last erased the history file." All of this computer lingo was spewed from the lips of a ten-year-old.

At the moment, her words were daggers in Jackie's heart. She felt like an idiot that didn't know anything about computers. She felt ignorant, old, unsophisticated. But she was blessed by this prodigy who grew up with computers. Tonight little Kimberly's words were tools in Jackie's arsenal. Bless the young – for they know not what they do or say.

Confident that her tracks were covered, Jackie once again headed for the bedroom. This time she crawled into bed with Roger and let exhaustion overtake her. She slept next to him that night because she needed more time to research and she did not need to raise any suspicion by sleeping in the guest room. Thankfully, she fell asleep immediately and the kids were shaking her shoulders asking for breakfast within a few hours. On this day she did not hear Roger get out of bed, get dressed or get out the door. How many times had he snuck out the door to do whatever it was he was doing? How many mornings had he left his kids and wife at home while he lived his other life? Every moment and every thought became a question that morning.

Jackie fed the kids and got them off to school and played the perfect mother at the bus stop. Her neighborhood buddies waited with their kids and chatted while gripping hot cups of coffee. Discussions of the new "in" restaurants continued as her mind raced with fear over what she would discover that day. For 20 minutes the bus stop friends chatted, as usual, about their weekends. Jane's kids had basketball camp, Marcie went to her cabin and Linda had a well-deserved babysitter for her twins. And Jackie? What did she do all weekend? "Well, this weekend was my dad's 65th birthday party. My sisters and brother came into town to celebrate," she said. "It was wonderful." The perfect family.

Good damn thing no one asked about Monday!

As discussions continued about who would drive the carpool to dance class or tennis lessons, Jackie's thoughts returned to websites and gay chat rooms. As Jackie walked home from the bus stop on that chilly but sunny Tuesday morning she was exhausted and pale from a lack of sleep. The bus stop friends commented on her lack of typical enthusiasm for discussion. "I had a hard night," was the only comment Jackie was willing to muster.

Returning to the house after a half hour of chatter, Jackie poured some coffee and got down to business. Hours flew by as she visited one potentially incriminating website after another. They all had ugly names like bigbadmuscle.com or menforsextoday.com. It sickened her, but she was on a roll. Out of ink…bummer. Off to Office Depot for supplies, then back to work. For three days this routine continued. For three days Jackie didn't remember eating lunch. The kids would have breakfast with her, but then she'd blink and it was time to make dinner.

Tuesday and Wednesday came and went. She slept in bed with Roger. This week really turned out to be a game…a game she created to judge herself on how well she was able to play. Fool the kids that she had a great day with friends – move ahead one space. Make a beautiful dinner and join in on "how was your day" conversation without missing a beat – get a free turn! Trick Roger into believing all is as normal – jump a space. Get all the information she needs to plan her attack on his cheating? Get out of jail free!

On Thursday, Roger called from work to say that he would be out of town for the night on business with a return on Friday. This routine was so commonplace that long ago Jackie had stopped asking him where he would be overnight. As salesmen often do, Roger often spent extended periods on the road or took unexpected trips "to close a deal." She had never given much thought to the ironic nature of the phrase "to close a deal" before.

Roger left for wherever he was going that evening and Jackie left for the comfort of the glass of wine she could count on finding somewhere in the neighborhood. Her gals – the most wonderful neighborhood of moms- were always up for a bump of wine or beer before making dinner for their families. It was a common activity to bring a bottle or two along with some glasses out into the yard around 5:00 p.m. to share with whoever stopped by.

Thankfully on this Thursday night, the warm breezes of fall and the beautiful colors of gold and red leaves created the perfect atmosphere for a patio party. Linda was already out on the front porch with at least six friends by the time Jackie joined the festivities. She was worn out from all her obsessive activities of the week. She drank a few beers, chatted about kids and movies and books, and crashed into bed completely engulfed in exhaustion.

# Discussion:

*The internet is a tool for discovery.*

Like Jackie, I turned to the internet to find information about the world of a gay husband. Googling "married gay men" led me to books like "My Husband is Gay -- A Woman's Guide to Surviving the Crisis" by Carol Grever and "The Other Side of the Closet -- the Coming Out Crisis for Straight Spouses and Families" by Amity Pierce Buxton, Ph.D. Little did I know at the time that these books would soon become my bibles. Jackie, Mary and Carol all own at least one of these books. Additional web searches brought me to organizations I had never heard of, including: Rainbow Families, PFLAG (Parents, Families and Friends of Lesbians and Gays), GAMMA (Gay and Married Men's Association), Gay Switchboard and The Gay and Lesbian Task Force.

The list goes on and on for support of gays and lesbians. I was grateful to find these resources, but interested in the fact that only one organization was narrowly focused and dedicated to helping the straight spouse: Straight Spouse Network.

Here is what the Straight Spouse Network says on their internet homepage (www.straightspouse .org):

*The Straight Spouse Network (SSN) is an international organization that provides personal, confidential support and information to heterosexual spouses/partners, current or former, of gay, lesbian, bisexual or transgender mates and mixed-orientation couples for constructively resolving coming-out problems. SSN also offers research-based information about spouse, couple, and family issues and resources to other family members, professionals, community organizations, and the public. SSN is the only support network of its kind in the world.*

The Straight Spouse Network is a fantastic organization that is supported by donations only. I encourage you to take advantage of their wonderful resources and support groups and to donate to them as you can.

The internet is likely to have unique appeal not only for us in our search for information, but also for our gay husbands. It is particularly popular with gay men because, like other disenfranchised or marginalized groups, they have relatively few places in which they can meet without fear of negative social consequences. Many men who are sexually attracted to men meet in traditional venues, such as gay organizations, gay bars and nightclubs, gay cultural events, saunas, beats, and via friends. However, over the past decade the internet has become a popular venue for gay men to exchange information, discuss political and other issues of interest, converse in chat rooms, place personal ads, and partake in cybersex fantasies (erotic discussions and fantasies online without any face-to-face contact) in an anonymous fashion without fear of reprisal.

If you suspect that your man has been on the internet surfing for information about how to hook up with another man, try checking your history file on your internet browser. If the previous user has not cleared the file, you will see a list of all the sites that have been visited in recent history.

If you suspect that your husband is listing himself on a gay dating website, you may consider searching for topics like "gay male dating," "gay men dating," "homosexual dating" or the like. Beware before you click on any of these sites that they may leave cookies on your computer that will allow users to know where you have been searching. I suggest clearing your computers of cookies after your search.

Prepare yourself for pornographic and sometimes violent material before you choose to enter any gay men's dating site. Many that I visited are full of total frontal and rear nudity. Some show men wearing leather harnesses in dungeon-esque settings. Some show sweet-looking young men (who seem to be younger than the required user age of 21) in vulgar positions with other men three times their age. I was completely unprepared for what I saw when I was writing this book. I have visited over 30 gay men's dating sites and I have seen things that I never thought I would see.

Now…let's be fair here. Most of the sites I speak about above could be regarded as pornographic. Many gay men dating sites exist that are blatantly sexual and downright ugly. Some sites like Chemistry.com and Mypartner.com seem classy and void of any erotic stereotypes, but look closely and you will find varying degrees of decency. Straight dating internet sites, like male gay dating sites, vary widely in their presentations.

Last year, I read a note from a mentor of mine encouraging women wanting to uncover their husbands' computer activity to invest $99.00 in spyware. For less than a conversation with a private detective, she said, you can get all the information you want to know—or more information than you probably want to know—off of your computer. And you will not leave any trace of your activities. Because of her suggestion I found a spyware company that allowed me to anonymously download a program that would tell me what anyone using our computer had been doing. The spyware program I used can be found and downloaded here: http://www.spectorsoft.com. If this site changes then search for the term "spyware" to find new purchasing resources.

For those of you who are considering employing this tactic, I want to make sure you know that downloading the spyware is the easy part. The hard part is being mentally prepared to find the information you think you want. Thinking it and confronting it are two very different issues. No matter how women ready themselves for the worst, and no matter how much they say that the information that will set them free, absorbing it can be quite painful. Be prepared for anything before you start trolling for evidence on your computer.

# 5 EXPLORING HIS SECRET WORLD

## Jackie

"What type of man would Roger look for?" Jackie asked herself. What does he want to see on these websites that he can't see at home? What has he been obsessed with lately that might help me understand who he wants to be?

Gotcha. She developed an identity of the person that she thought Roger would be interested in. By opening a free e-mail account she had the tool to infiltrate the gay dating websites. All she had to do was pretend to be someone else. She could use her internet identity to become a man who would entice her husband to come out of hiding.

*Mrracketsport*, the man she created in cyber space, was a tall, well built, athletic, good-looking, smart, articulate, versatile, available, anonymous, clean, HIV- negative man who lived in upstate New York and traveled frequently to Roger's city on business. He wore a suit during the day and was into anonymous encounters. He was a member of a popular gay men's dating site.

*Mrracketsport* gave Jackie access to the secret world of gay men personals online. *Mrracketsport,* her new online identity, allowed her to search for men based on a number of criteria ranging from hair color or height, to HIV status. A quick search for men in her area who possessed similar physical qualities to Roger developed a list of 57 men. After close scrutiny of each and every contestant she sighed deeply with relief and caught her breath. Roger wasn't here.

After a moment of relaxation, Jackie got back to the task at hand. She does not give up easily. "What am I missing?" she kept asking herself. She listened to that voice in her soul that told her Roger was on this website. But why couldn't she find him? "Think like Roger," she told herself. "Be like Roger." Then it came to her. If she was to be Roger, then she had to answer the question "Who am I?"

She revised her search criteria. The mistake she made the first time around was creating a search based on Roger's actual identity. This time, she chose search criteria based on what she was learning about the social world of these websites. The social world of online gay dating is not unlike the world of heterosexual e-dating. Most users lie about their age and everyone would love to date someone attractive or rich.

Bingo.

She found him. She found him with a search that included men ranging from 35 years of age to 44 years of age. Roger was 40 at the time so her preliminary search for him included men from the age of 40 to 46 years of age. How silly of her! Of course Roger was 39 in his head. He was also not gray-haired or married!

She opened his personal ad and saw a photo of Roger. She threw up all over her fluffy robe. She took a deep breath and she threw up again.

It was now 3:00 a.m. and her body shook from the loss of electrolytes from crying for the past two hours. She shuddered at the horror of what lay before her in her office, on the computer. She was bathed in vomit and angry as hell. It was not a pretty sight. But there was much more work to be done, so she cleaned up her surroundings, took a quick shower and got back into bed with her husband. Fear can make you do strange things.

The next morning she watched Roger leave for work with a fire burning through her soul. Somehow she got the kids fed and off to school. She returned from the bus stop to spend the rest of the day on the task at hand. She did not eat breakfast nor lunch, did not take breaks, and did not throw up again. She was on a mission to gather as much evidence as she could before she formed a plan of how to approach Roger.

This scenario played itself out for three days. Jackie printed every piece of information that she could find on the net. She stored every piece of evidence in a file and hid it in the Christmas ornaments where no one would look. She became obsessed with producing evidence of his infidelity.

Jackie ran through four cartridges of ink on her printer that week. She copied every bank statement on her joint account for the last three years. She copied every Visa statement, every investment statement and every financial document that could produce any hint of evidence that she may need in the future. To this day, she wishes she had copied even more.

While Roger was at work and the kids were at school, Jackie scoured her home for clues to his secret life. She became a crazy woman. She opened every drawer, every shoebox, every pocket and every piece of luggage that Roger owned. What she found were pieces of a puzzle that had existed for many years. Without her latest revelation on the internet she still believes she would have never put together the pieces of this puzzle to create the picture of Roger's hidden life.

## Mary

When Mary found out that her husband was taking HIV medication, she wondered when he had contracted the disease. She still did not know that Jeff was a gay man, only that he was infected with a life-threatening virus that he contracted from someone other than her.

Her path to discovery was a terrible journey that started with the HIV pills. Mary contacted the clinic in South Carolina from which he received shipment of his medicines. She pretended to be an office worker at her insurance company. She asked the billing office if they had received payment for her husband's prescription. The center indicated that the prescription was paid for in cash. This time it was Mary's turn to feel sick.

Moments later she perused her checking account and found unexplained withdrawals of over $400 that had occurred monthly for the previous year. She never asked Jeff about his monetary withdrawals because they trusted each other with the family money. In reality, Mary was lucky that the drugs did not cost a lot more. It is common for HIV medications to cost in the thousands of dollars per month.

Terrified about what she might hear, Mary then called their life insurance company. Had Jeff's life insurance policy been altered due to his physical condition? She was happy to hear that his policy was paid in full and current. Unfortunately, upon reading the policy, she assumed that paying the policy was a waste of money. There were a number of clauses in the contract that she thought would allow the insurance company to void the contract due to his HIV status. She wanted clarification, but she was too ashamed to call her lawyer with an inquiry.

So instead she worried.

A complete search of her home and Jeff's car and his briefcase led Mary to the discovery of a life full of cheating activities. Jeff had been using a free hotmail account to keep in contact with his liaisons and had created quite a collection of sex toys that Mary found in the spare wheel well of his car.

The worst part of Mary's story is how despondent she became over the welfare of her children. Could Jeff have infected their son when he cut himself while working on the car this summer? Could their daughter have the disease from goodnight kisses with Dad? Even after educating herself about HIV and AIDS online, Mary worried continuously about whether Jeff would make them all sick. She felt imprisoned by his lack of disclosure.

## Carol

When Greg brought satellite TV and internet service into the home, Carol quickly realized that something had changed in her husband. He rapidly grew addicted to the computer, spending hours and hours alone surfing the net. After she would go to bed, Greg would often stay up until early the next morning watching TV.

Carol was a lovely woman and she loved the quiet life that rural America offered. She did not have a cell phone and she was content to be ignorant about computers. Her discovery of her husband's change in sexual orientation came from the magazines that started arriving at her home. First there was a catalog for fancy shirts and slacks. Then a catalog for sexy men's underwear showed up. Eventually she could not ignore the barrage of periodicals with young handsome men on the cover.

"What is going on?" she begged of Greg.

"There must be some mistake" he said. "Those magazines that you order clothes from must have sold our name to some mail list company."

# Discussion:
*Why should you document your discovery process?*


When I became aware that my husband may be gay, I was like Jackie; curious – no, tormented. My inquiring mind raged at first, like Jackie's, since I knew nothing about homosexual activities. I spent hours and hours on the internet looking for any clues that would give me a glimpse into his world. I went to the bookstore and bought every piece of literature I could on any related subject. I spent my days immersed in educating myself about everything from the meaning of the Latin prefix "homo" to what the term "bareback" means. I was literally obsessed. Eventually my curiosity for the bizarre calmed down and I felt more centered. My curiosity of his lifestyle moved slowly from intense and unreasonable to questioning and understanding.

For me, information was my coping drug of choice. It was the tool that allowed me to rationally begin the process of healing.

For Mary, reliving the past was necessary to get a handle on how she would treat the future. For her, memory was a powerful tool. Memories haunted her, like the day Mary's ten-year-old son discovered a picture of a naked man on her fax. This happened about three months prior to the camping trip during which her son found drugs in the tent. Mary's husband Jeff dismissed the fax as a terrible, unsolicited item. Then there was the time, about six months before, when Mary opened her PC to find an AOL e-mail account under the signature of Jaxsir. Mary remembers asking Jeff if he knew who Jaxsir was. He replied that AOL must have screwed up his account. And lastly, she remembers finding a thick, metal ring in his sock drawer. She asked him what the purpose of this device was. He mentioned that he had bought it as a sexual device to enhance her pleasure. She never experienced the use of that device.

Denial can also be a powerful force. Mary was unaware, until much further into the process of divorce, how she had allowed her naïveté to shield her from things she didn't want to know. Faxes of naked men do not just arrive on your doorstep. E-mail accounts with strange names do not just appear on your PC. Solid silver rings are not used to enhance sexual pleasure for a female (well maybe they are...but Mary has yet to understand how). All four of us women can note times when we brushed off our keen senses of betrayal in order to continue the fairytales we thought we were living.

For Carol, denial delayed her discovery process. She refused to accept that Greg's erratic behavior had nothing to do with her. She tried for years to "fix" their dwindling sex life and she lost her self-esteem, her friends, and her close ties with family and people who cared for her. She let Greg's selfish actions change her into someone she did not want to be. She grew despondent and lonely.

As Jackie, Mary and I look back at the roads that led us to the discovery of our gay husbands, to the destruction of our marriages and finally to our recoveries, we all wish we had done one thing along the way: kept a journal. We wish we had taken the time to write the stories of our lives down on paper. When all hell broke loose in my divorce, I wish I had the benefit of consistent memories to back up my narratives. With fear and anger as driving forces, memories jumble and timelines are skewed.

Jackie is plagued with worry that she is not remembering things the way they really happened.

To this day she questions whether she was so anxious to divorce Roger that she was untrue to herself in the financial outcome of the process.

Carol has kept a journal, although not consistently, for most of her adult life. The journals she wrote during the process of her husband's "coming out" and those that she kept throughout her marriage helped her realize that she was not at fault for her husband's actions. Carol's therapist encouraged her to review her journals as she walked her path to recovery. She felt encouragement as she looked back on her personal records and realized that she had done all she could to stem the tide of decline in her marriage. She read about the slow but consistent loss of sexual relations in her relationship. She read about the feelings of sorrow she had when her husband's activities made her withdraw from her community. She read about the fear she felt and the courage she summoned to confront Greg.

All of us agree that a woman should keep a journal. It is a loving gift we give to ourselves. Writing and expressing our thoughts on paper can heal us. It can focus, support and enhance our lives and our well-being. Whether we laugh or we cry, whether through sorrow or joy, we can understand more about ourselves and each other through keeping a journal.

**Some benefits of keeping a journal include:**

- Stress reduction – By keeping track of events we feel more organized.

- Goal setting – In times of high stress, making clear and consistent goals can help you feel more in control of your life structure.

- Organization – Managing your thoughts on paper releases frustration.

- Helps focus – Taking time for activities like journaling helps people focus on what is important to them in their own lives.

- Improves well-being – Journaling about throwing books at my walls in frustration allowed me to release anger and become calmer.

- Makes time for you – During a divorce or during periods of great stress it is common to forget to take care of oneself. Stopping to write in a journal is a good way to carve out some "me time."

- Creates a personal reminder – We can always use a little help in remembering life's details.

I should have kept a journal during the tough times that followed the discovery of my husband's homosexuality; however, the overwhelming thought of doing one more thing a day kept me from writing things down.

What I should have done is bought a voice recorder. While driving in my car, I often had glimpses of the past and memories which I would have liked to have written down. By the time I drove to my destination I had forgotten the thought. I suggest you buy one of those little digital voice recorders and keep it in your purse or car for recording random thoughts. Often the compilation of these thoughts can provide a more precise story for your journal, or for a lawyer, should you need it in your divorce proceedings.

Olympus makes great digital voice recorders that sell for as little as $50. They are small and incredibly convenient to use. You can record your voice and then just insert the special USB hookup on the device to your computer and download your recording into any media file. Then you can e-mail it or keep it in a "if needed for divorce" file.

The main thing is this: pay attention to little clues that your man is giving you about his life. Write them down! Be like the forensic gals on the hit show CSI (Crime Scene Investigations). Allow the clues to come to you and somehow store every one. Write them in a journal or record them on tape. Every detail may not make sense today, but eventually it will add up to a story. You may need these clues in divorce court. You may need the clues to write your own story. You may need the clues to strengthen your case for collecting alimony or child support. Remember this: you are not the one to blame here. Keeping track of his activities and what he says is not vindictive. It is not unkind. It is survival, and it is necessary. Whatever they may be...write down the clues!

# 6   THE CONFRONTATION

## *Jackie*

When she finally had enough evidence to approach Roger, Jackie started to lay the foundation of a plan to confront him. She set up a dinner appointment on Friday and called Roger to suggest that they have a "date night." He was receptive and they decided to meet at 7:00 p.m. She was terrified, but determined to find out why she had been betrayed for so long and why Roger would do this to her.

"I needed to feel powerful and in control for this meeting," she told me. "I was terrified and mad and lonely. And I was sick." Staying up until 4:00 a.m. for the past couple of nights had left Jackie coughing and with a fever. She felt so awful, in fact, that she almost cancelled her plans to confront Roger. "Buck up," she remembers telling herself.

She decided that she felt the most powerful when she

wore her business suits, so she told Roger that she had business downtown and that she would meet him at a chic restaurant named La Francais. He fell for the story.

By 5:30 p.m. she was dressed to kill in her strongest black knock 'em dead Ann Taylor suit and sitting at the pub across the street from La Francais having a glass of wine. The first chardonnay took her three minutes to inhale. The second drink took a minute or two more. A woman on a mission… that was Jackie.

She sat in the bar with the backpack that she put together for Roger. Inside the pack were a t-shirt, jeans, toothbrush and sneakers that she had packed for him. He would surely ask her what the backpack was for. She was prepared to say it was some work material. He would find out soon enough that it was for him.

A few glasses of wine helped her feel less stressed. She sat in that bar and ran through the night in her head: how she would meet Roger at the bar, have benign conversation about his hectic week, and then be seated at a table where they would enjoy a nice dinner. Then, right before the dessert, she would ask, "What the heck have you been doing for the past couple of years, Roger?" She had run through the scenario in her head one hundred times.

She brought a book so that she would not have to look at other people while she concocted her plan. She sipped chardonnay at the bar, unresponsive to the kind bartender who graciously asked if she was ok as she started to cry. He handed her a tissue. She felt like she was the distraught brunette in a television show ordering shots to take the pain away. Jackie had never been good at drinking shots, but the chardonnay was working its magic, and she felt a blanket of calm surrounding her.

In bars like this one, there are always free regional newspapers that you can pick up at the door. Jackie had snapped up one on her way in. She turned to the paper. *City Pages* was a hip rag full of cool people and "in" happenings in the area. As karma would have it, she opened it up to a page about gay bars. The article was full of lewd references to "bests." Best place to pick up a lover…best place for hotties…best whatever.

Finding out your man is gay is a little like being pregnant. It is something you never really think about until it happens to you. And when it happens to you, it seems like it is also happening to everyone else. Prior to Jackie's discovery of Roger's second life, she never really thought about gay men. Now they were everywhere!

Jackie finished her second glass of wine and thanked God that it was almost 7:00 p.m. Time to get to the restaurant and start talking. She put on her coat to ward off the crisp October air, and headed down the busy downtown streets to the restaurant. Why did she feel that she needed to wear three inch heels for this meeting? Sure, she looked great. Sure, she was empowered. But her feet hurt like hell. Her toes were frozen and her back hurt and she was pissed. God forbid any stray person on the street should happen to get in her way.

The evening was chilly – maybe 40 degrees. There were no stars in the sky. Clouds shrouded the streets with a misty blanket that chilled your bones. By the time she got to the front door, she was cold and wet and her hair, which she had taken extra time to style, looked like the fur on a golden retriever after retrieving a dead duck from a lake. Okay, maybe it was not that bad…but she was not feeling her sexiest and most radiant.

The atmosphere in the restaurant was a welcome contrast to the dreariness of the street. Inside, the lights were dim and seductive, the colors were rich and warm, and the beautiful people were busy talking and having a nice time. "Good thing I wore my heels," Jackie remembers thinking as she entered the bar. Every female in the joint was dressed in either a fabulous business suit or a slinky evening dress. And high heels.

Roger was already at the bar when she sauntered in. As usual, she noticed him immediately. It was hard not to. Roger is a big man with a full head of thick salt and pepper hair, and is stunning. "What a waste," she thought the moment she saw him. "What a waste for the female race that you are gay."

Jackie used to love showing up to events with Roger because he is so beautiful. She used to love watching other women watch him. She used to love walking into a room with him because he always had his arm around her back. He was the husband who always got her a drink, pulled out her chair to sit down, and stood up when she went to the ladies' room. His mother taught him well how to be a good husband. Tonight, she would tell him he was no longer wanted.

A flood of tears overtook Jackie as she glanced at him across the bar. She wanted to scream and cry and rant. She wanted to close her eyes and rewind time and go back to her comfortable, inviting home with their kids and the cat snuggled up on the couch watching movies. She wanted all the pain to go away.

Jackie dug deep inside and instructed herself to get focused. "Get it together girl."

The talk worked. It took maybe 30 seconds to get out of "I love you and long for you" mode into "you better be ready because I am going to bury you" mode. Jackie put a new layer of lipstick on, summoned her courage, and walked through the stylish bar to the handsome guy in the back who just happened to be her homosexual husband.

After a warm greeting, Roger put their names on the list for a table to have dinner. Damn it – she forgot that this place was one of the most popular restaurants in the city. Dinner would be at least a 45 minute wait. On a typical night, they might consider taking a quick walk to another restaurant. Roger looked at her with a "Well, what would you like to do?" look.

"We'll be waiting at the bar," she told the maitre d'. So off to the bar they went, in search of a section of couch or a small bar table to sit and talk about the day. Fortunately, Jackie and Roger grabbed a great spot on a couch by the window. Jackie's chardonnay arrived expeditiously, as did Roger's martini. Roger always ordered a martini on nights when he was comfortable and ready to get a quick buzz.

Jackie decided not to bring up the subject at hand until she and Roger were safely seated at a table and she could control the situation. With this in mind, she spent the next half an hour jabbering with Roger about whatever came up, and watching him like a hawk to see if he was checking out other men. He never even glanced at another guy. He was good. He was focused. He was talking to her and only her. In fact, he was strangely focused on her and her great suit and her pretty makeup. The compliments were many and free-flowing. She was actually comfortable and relaxed in this mindless banter. Jackie sipped her wine slowly, as the two she had had in the previous bar were catching up to her and taking their toll on her clear thinking.

Just as they got up from the plush blue sofa to be seated at a table, Roger noticed the backpack that Jackie was carrying. "Why on Earth do you have our son's backpack tonight?"

She wanted to say, "Because it is full of your lying, son-of-a-bitch pajamas that you will wear in some ugly hotel room tonight because you are a jerk." Instead, she answered, "Oh, it is full of work stuff, and I forgot to put it in the car." Thank goodness the subject was dropped as they sat at a small, two-person table tucked away near the windows. There were people around them, but it was quiet enough and private enough for a potentially volatile conversation.

Jackie's father had offered to be her escort during her upcoming confrontation with Roger. Her dad had mentioned that she should not be alone when confronting Roger. "You never know how he might react," Jackie remembers him saying. "He may get angry and hurt you." But Roger had never raised a hand to her. In fact, he and Jackie had never even had a real argument. "Roger would never hit me," she remembers thinking. But did she really know Roger?

Jackie's father's words guided her strategy for the evening. If they were in public, Roger would never hit her. Roger was handsome, but he was also vain. In a crowded restaurant, he would also never raise his voice or yell at her. That would be "inappropriate." This table in this chic establishment was all the protection she needed to expose her findings.

They sat down at a sweet little table and carried on with benign conversation for a few minutes. They ordered dinner. Jackie ordered food that was not fussy or difficult to eat. She was sure that she would eat very little of whatever was on the plate, so she opted for a caramelized onion and goat cheese pizza. Roger ordered pasta.

After the semantics of ordering food, she got down to the business at hand.

"Roger," she said with a quivering voice.

"Yes?"

"We need to talk about something."

There was no sign that he was aware of what she would say next. Jackie took a deep breath and blurted it out.

"If you want to be a gay man then go ahead and do it, but stop hiding in the comfort and stability of our marriage."

Silence.

Roger looked at Jackie from across the table and did something that made her furious. He should have been crying and begging for forgiveness and mercy and telling her how sorry he was. He should have been sobbing in regret. Instead, he sat looking at her and he did…nothing. For 60 seconds, which seemed like an eternity, he did nothing. An additional minute passed. Nothing. Jackie resisted the temptation to freak out and hit him. He did not cry. He did not wail. He did not get up and scream. He did absolutely nothing.

"Well?" she finally said, uncomfortable with the silence.

Nothing.

Finally a word. "What?."

"What do you mean, what?" is all she could muster.

"What did you just say?" he mumbled somewhat incoherently. No tears, no emotion.

"Damn. I'm going to have to say it again!" Jackie thought. After all the rehearsals in her head it was not difficult to come up with exactly the same words she said a minute ago.

"If you want to be a gay man then go ahead and do it, but

stop hiding in the comfort and stability of our marriage."

Jackie was so angry at Roger that she wanted to scream it out for the whole joint to hear. Finally, the words that she had been practicing for a week were coming out of her mouth. She was proud of herself. She gave herself a mental pat on the back and continued her silent stare.

"So this is how it's going to go down," he said.

This time it was Jackie's turn for clarification. "What the hell does that mean?" she asked.

"So this is how it's going to go down," he repeated.

"You tell me, Roger. Is this how it's going to go down?"

Roger stopped, finally, and his face lost all color.

"What do you know?" he inquired.

"What the hell should I know?" The cat and mouse game of information was pissing her off, and if history repeats itself, then he would win this stupid game. Roger always had a way of outsmarting Jackie in the little dramas that happen in relationships…but she had the element of surprise on her side, and she was not going to waste the opportunity.

"Roger – I can't even start to tell you how disappointed and frustrated and angry and hurt and pissed I am at you. Right now I want to kill you. I want to string you up to a tree and throw rocks at you. I want…."

"Oh my God," he mumbled, "this isn't how it is supposed to happen."

Jackie decided to shut up and see where Roger was going with this thought. "This isn't how I thought it would end."

And at that very moment Jackie knew that this was, in fact, the beginning of the end.

The evening morphed into a question and answer session that Jackie wishes she had on tape. She remembers the parts when he finally cried and said how sorry he was. She remembers the parts when he begged her to not tell anyone. But she doesn't remember the part when he said "I was wrong in the way I treated you," or "I was wrong to put you at such risk," or "I was wrong to have lied for the last couple of years." Jackie is pretty sure she doesn't remember such phrases because they were never spoken.

To end their discussion, Jackie handed Roger the backpack and told him to find a hotel for the night. It was empowering to throw it at him, to be the one in control. The control lasted for two minutes until Jackie fell back into the comfortable role of submissive spouse and gave in to his begging to return to their house for the evening. He would sleep in the guest bedroom. Looking back, it sickens Jackie that she allowed him to come back home that night.

Roger convinced Jackie that she should let him stay in the home while they figured out the "best" way to tell the kids. He stayed in the house, sleeping in the guest bedroom for the next six weeks, so that they could have one last Thanksgiving and Christmas as a family. During this time, Roger and Jackie experienced an awakened feeling of closeness. They often talked until late in the evening about what he had experienced in his journey to this point. He was open and honest about many of the details of his story. At the time Jackie was lonely, afraid and curious. She listened to many hours of details because it made her feel closer to him. She and Roger bonded again over discussions of their past and possible future. She asked question after question:

"What was the first time you remember knowing that you were gay?"

"What did you do on all the 'guy trips' with your friends?"

"How do you know if someone else is gay? Can you pick someone out at the airport and just know that he's gay?"

"What caused you to go trolling on the internet?"

"Why did you not just tell me?"

"What happened that made you snap?"

"Were you gay when you married me?"

Roger told Jackie of countless times that he had repressed his feelings of homosexuality due to family or religious reasons, in hopes that he could make them disappear. They talked of the good times in their marriage, and created preparations for their eventual separation. They made plans for finding appropriate counseling and help telling the kids. They even discussed the makings of their amicable divorce.

The actual details of Jackie and Roger's divorce vary significantly from the idyllic path they discussed, but Jackie does think that those weeks of tearful and gut-wrenching discussions helped her and her husband better understand the other's perspective

For some couples, sharing a huge secret like the coming out of a spouse creates a bond of sympathy and compassion for a period of time after the disclosure. This is more likely to occur when there has been honest love and companionship in the relationship. As much as partners try to sustain it, however, the glow of a return to intimacy lasts only a short while.

## *Mary*

When Mary and Jeff got married they were as poor as church mice. They struggled financially at first due to student loans and entry level jobs. They shared a car, rented a small apartment and clipped coupons to feed themselves. They worked well as partners to create a modest yet loving home. The couple decided early in their marriage that each would continue working while raising their family. Jeff had set up a system that would put most of his earnings into accounts meant to fund their retirement. Mary's income was used for household expenses, including the mortgage.

As time passed the couple had two children and each spouse continued to climb the corporate ladder. At first they were successful at combining careers and family, however as their job stresses increased, so did the tension in the household.

As Jeff became more successful at work he demanded an "upgrade" in their lifestyle. He moved the family into a bigger home and bought new cars. He started wearing custom made shirts and Italian suits. He convinced Mary to put the kids in private schools. Their friends and neighbors thought that Jeff and Mary had it made.

Then Jeff lost his job. He earned far less on his replacement job, and he succumbed to the stress by consuming alcohol and becoming reclusive and angry. Jeff slowly went from being an easy-going boyfriend to successful loving husband to a stressed out, vodka-drinking father.

Mary felt the change in her husband for years before her son found the drugs in his luggage. She tried to talk to Jeff about why he was spending so much time at work. She begged him to pay more attention to the kids. She even scheduled a sitter for "date night" every Friday. Nothing worked. Jeff slowly retreated from his family. Mary thought that maybe he was having an affair. It was not until the discovery of the drugs that Mary knew her husband was having sex outside their marriage.

On a Tuesday night after the kids went to bed, Mary confronted Jeff with her findings. As he sat on the couch, she told him about their son's discovery and about her investigation. She told him she knew about the clinic in South Carolina that serviced his prescription for HIV medication. She told him she had been tested and that the rapid tests for HIV were negative. She told him that she was so very sorry about his HIV status. She told him that she was sorry that he felt he had to lie about his condition. Then she asked him if he was having an affair.

When Jeff told Mary that he had been involved with someone for almost a year, she cried. When he told her he was involved with another man she screamed. Mary was so angry and bewildered that she could not speak. She threw Jeff out of the house that night. He, of course, had somewhere to go. He never said he was sorry for deceiving her. He offered her no apology for putting her at risk for a life-threatening disease. He did not offer any explanation for his actions. He left the house and never returned to live at the home again.

## Carol

After years of sadness, disconnection and fear, Carol left Greg. She had grown despondent over the loss of any sexual or emotional connection with her husband. She had become so very lonely in her marriage that she knew it could not be saved. When she begged Greg to tell her what was happening to him, he told her she was crazy. Greg told Carol that the loss of their sex life was due to her inability to please him. He told her that he had spent hours and hours a day on the internet because she was boring. He, like many gay married men before him, led his wife to believe that the loss of social connection in his marriage was her fault.

Carol's family had begged her to leave him. When she finally did leave the home, she told no one about the magazines and the male porn items that arrived in the mail. Carol never told anyone that Greg was gay. Even though she knew he had deceived her, she felt so sorry for him that she did not dare reveal his secret.

For the following months and years, Greg continued a life of seclusion alone in the home Carol left. He divorced her, but he feared being "outed" in the divorce proceedings. Carol, too, was afraid of how the community would treat her if Greg's homosexuality was revealed. Her husband's sexual orientation broke the code of the community's mores and she felt like she would be stigmatized along with Greg if people found them out. The fear of what would happen to them kept both Carol and Greg inside the closet until Greg died 4 years later. Carol's husband never came out publicly and she never told any of her friends about his hidden life. She keeps all their secrets to this day.

# Discussion:
*How do you find the "right" divorce lawyer?*

After the confrontation or revelation, the most common action taken in mixed orientation marriages is divorce. Studies show that in 85 percent of cases, the revelation that one spouse is gay leads to divorce. In only 15 percent of cases, the marriage continues. This is usually for financial and social reasons, with the straight spouse often climbing into the closet as well, to save face for family, friends and business associates.

No one ever wants to have to hire a divorce lawyer, but should divorce be in your future, you owe it to yourself and your children to hire the best attorney you can find and afford. First and foremost, listen to your instincts when searching for a lawyer. Really try to get a gut feeling if this attorney will be "right" for you and your case. You just may be spending more time with this person than you ever dreamed you would!

For example, think about whether a lawyer makes eye contact with you, and if not, whether this bothers you. Is the lawyer glib, dismissive, or callous or does he/she seem to have a real interest in you and your case?

The following list of attorney interview questions is provided by the Separated Parenting Access & Resource Center. I have added a few caveats to some of the questions that make them more relevant to the particular needs of a straight spouse. SPARC suggests you print out this list of questions and take it with you to your first meeting with a prospective lawyer. Just go right down the list, point by point. Take notes of the attorney's answers to each question. This will save a lot of confusion later and allow you to easily compare the answers you get from each attorney.

1. How long have you been practicing in this court, district or county?

2. What percentage of your practice is in Family Law, specifically in divorce and custody cases?

3. Have you ever represented a client who was in a divorce due to the changing of sexual orientation of one of the spouses?**

** My advice here is to NOT divulge which spouse is gay. See how your interviewee responds. I used this question when interviewing lawyers for my divorce. It turned out to be the defining question in my search because my lawyer answered "Yes, I have experience in representing clients whose marriages are ending due to the coming out of one of the spouses. I will tell you this…if you are the spouse who came out in your marriage then I am NOT the attorney for you. If it was your husband, however, then I am absolutely the attorney for you." I hired her because of that answer.

4. How do you feel about taking cases to a jury? What percentage of your cases have gone to a trial by jury?

5. Are you aware the Child Support guidelines are a rebuttable presumption?

6. Are you familiar with the judges in this county, in particular Judge XXXXXX? (The last part of this question would only apply if you know in advance who your judge will be. Depending on local court practices, you may or may not be able to find out who the judge will be.)

    a. If so, what are his/her "preferences" when dealing with a custody case? In other words, is he/she open to taking custody from a father who shares parenting responsibilities and giving custody to a mother as the custodial parent?

b. Is he/she open to awarding Joint Custody in the true sense of the word?

c. Does he/she usually prefer Parenting/Custody Evaluations?

7. What is your normal hourly rate?

8. Should I decide to hire you, would you be willing to sign a contract that as my lawyer, you will not take any action without my permission, unless circumstances are so urgent that there is no way to reach me for consultation, and that under no circumstances will you bind me to any agreement?

9. Should I decide to hire you, I would request the following:

a. The ability to communicate with you via e-mail.

b. The opportunity to some tasks myself in order to keep my costs down.

c. A complete and thorough brief, before submission, for any motions to be submitted or responded to with references to any case law, or other research used to make your reply.

d. A complete and thorough itemized billing of any and all billable work completed on my behalf.

e. When research is completed on my behalf and listed on the itemized bill, I wish to receive references as to where the research was done and what information pertaining to my case was obtained.

f.  The ability to hire you by your hourly rate with 5 hours paid upfront.

## After the particulars of your case are discussed:

1.  How long do you foresee this case taking?

2.  What would be your best estimate on the final costs?

3.  What do you feel my chances are of getting full custody, joint custody, increased time, etc?

## Hiring the Divorce Lawyer:

If the lawyer you're considering hiring didn't provide you with a copy of his or her standard contract at your interview, you should ask for one. Make sure you really understand the contract before you sign it. Also, be sure you understand the financial terms a lawyer is offering you. It comes as a shock to many legal customers when they learn that they are billed by the minute for talking on the phone to their lawyer and for their lawyer's talking on the phone to the other side's lawyer. Other items to keep in mind:

- **Obtaining an Action Plan**: Once your marital problems have risen to the level of a court case with lawyers involved, you will find yourself feeling like a passenger in a small rubber raft, floating with the current. Re-visit your action plan often with your lawyer. Try to get consistent information about where your case is moving and what to expect for timelines.

- **Sticking with a Plan**: A lawyer may have every intention of being assertive, aggressive and in control of the litigation and then, for whatever reason, fail to deliver on that promise. Keep consistent tabs on your lawyer to make sure he/she is consistently working on your behalf per your contract. If you feel that he/she is not giving your case the effort you deserve, consider changing lawyers or at least outline your concerns in a (short) letter to your attorney asking for focus.

**Communication with Your Lawyer:**

- ***Tell the Whole Truth and Provide Requested Information Promptly***: If your lawyer asks you for information, he or she will be stalled until you provide it.

- ***Have a Legitimate Reason to Call Your Lawyer:*** The stress of a divorce, and especially the behavior of your spouse, can put you on edge. Don't call your lawyer to chat – remember all your conversations are expensive! Call only when you have important information to discuss.

- ***Keep a Written Record of Everything:*** Events will occur that you might think are legally insignificant but are not. Keep a note pad in your car or purse and write anything down that may be important.

- ***Keep Your Account Current:*** Legal representation is not something you are entitled to. It is a service you must pay for, just as you pay for food, clothing, utilities, and car repairs. Pay on time and your lawyer may be more willing to work with you.

- ***Be Polite:*** Common sense tells you to be polite to your lawyer, but as your case goes on, you may find this difficult.

**Common Client Mistakes:**

- ***Succumbing to the Other Side's Mental Engineering:*** Another common mistake you must not make is to allow the other side's head games to bother you.

- ***Becoming Discouraged:*** Now that you have read something about how a divorce progresses, you can probably see the similarities between a divorce and many other challenges. Hang in there through the tough times. Find support from friends and family that will keep you from wanting to just give it all up.

- ***Using Your Lawer as a Therapist:*** Many times, you will be tempted to talk to your lawyer about your personal problems, particularly since he or she is right in the middle of the action.

- ***Expecting to Get Justice by Going to Court:*** Many people naively believe that, if they can just get the judge to listen to what their ex did, the judge will make things okay. Well, it doesn't always work that way. Most good lawyers, in my opinion, will encourage you to come to an agreement with your spouse outside of divorce court, if at all possible.

# 7    AFTER THE SHOCK

## *Jackie*

After a year full of anxiety and frustration, Jackie's divorce was well under way. Her lawyer had drawn up numerous renditions of a Marital Termination Agreement, and Roger and she had finally agreed on one. Roger promised her the agreement would be signed before he left for a ten-day vacation so that her lawyer could submit it to a judge. She was chomping at the bit to get this final phase of the divorce over with.

To celebrate the signing of the documents, Roger went on a cruise and Jackie went to the doctor.

The one year anniversary of Roger's forced "coming out" was upon her, and Jackie chose to celebrate by having her final HIV test. Due to the absence of sexual activity she had post-marriage, Jackie was not at all concerned with the outcome of the test. The nurse who drew her blood, however, gave her something new to be concerned about. As she stuck Jackie with a needle and asked her all the routine questions of a blood draw, she took Jackie's breath away with an offhand question..

"So, what type of language did you use in your divorce decree about your ex-husband and HIV?" she asked as though she were asking what Jackie planned to make for dinner.

"What do you mean?" she shyly responded.

"Well," she continued "your chart says that your husband is gay and is sexually active. Right?"

"Right," she answered, wondering where this line of questioning was leading.

"Well," she continued without interruption, "if Roger may have more than one sexual partner, he runs a higher than normal risk of contracting HIV and other diseases which may be not only dangerous, but life threatening." Then she asked "Do you know if he has HIV?"

Jackie stopped in her tracks. The last time she had talked to Roger about HIV was a year earlier, just prior to her first test. She had been so focused on her own physical well-being that she had not even considered asking Roger about his HIV status. This was low on her list of concerns at her six-month test, and even lower at her one-year test. She had no idea if Roger had contracted HIV or any other sexually transmitted diseases. She had no idea what Roger's sexual activity level had been for the last year. In fact, she was proud to admit that she was rarely thinking about Roger's escapades.

"You should ask him," said the nurse "and you should know if he ever contracts HIV. You should talk about how you will discuss HIV with your kids if either of you should ever contract it."

What if Roger had HIV? What if he should contract it? She finished her exam and called her lawyer who promptly advised her to discuss this with Roger. Then she suggested strongly that they put language into the divorce decree about how they would approach this issue with the kids.

Jackie spent the three nights prior to Roger's return from his vacation, worrying about how they would talk to the kids about HIV. Like she didn't have enough to worry about already.

## Mary

Immediately after learning about Jeff's HIV medication, Mary got herself tested. She went to the public clinic that she and her girlfriends had visited in college to get birth control. Of course she did not reveal her activities to anyone, and she succumbed to her worries and stress by becoming distraught and sick. The wonderful nurses at the health clinic informed her of her chances of contracting HIV, and tried to soothe her worries by telling her about the many effective medications available. They were wonderful...but until she had lived HIV-free for a year, Mary suffered headaches, nausea, back-pain and numerous other ailments due to the stress.

## Carol

Carol has never been tested for HIV. The fear of finding out she may have contracted the disease from the man to whom she had been married for so many years was too much for her to bear. And if she did have HIV...she would surely be shunned by her conservative neighbors and friends. Instead of counting on doctors to tell her she was fine, Carol returned to the deep seated faith in God that she had relied on so many years ago. She asked her God to take care of her. In her heart, she was confident that she was not infected with any sexually transmitted diseases. Ten years after her husband died Carol remains disease free. Emotionally she has paid a big price for her decision to not be tested. She had many years of worry. Today she looks back with regret that she did not have the courage to take tests that would have set her worry aside...but at the time she just could not emotionally deal with the potential that Greg would have given her a life threatening disease.

## Discussion:
*What exactly are HIV/AIDS and STD tests...and what's the big deal?*

When a straight spouse realizes how risky her home life is, depending on the nature of her husband's outside sexual activity, she usually hurries, as I did, to a medical clinic or public health center for an HIV/AIDS test. Good! Any woman who has had sexual relations with her husband - who may have had sexual relations with another person - is at risk of being exposed to HIV and other sexually transmitted diseases. She should immediately find out the truth about her own health. For any woman who has had sexual relations with a sexually active gay man, the importance of AIDS and STD testing cannot be overstressed.

In my own experience, I was terrified to go to my gynecologist to get an HIV/AIDS test. Like Jackie, I was ashamed to be there, and I was nervous to tell the nurses who had taken care of me since my babies were born about why I was getting an

AIDS test. I also knew nothing about how the test would be performed or how I would receive the results. To make your visit easier than mine, here is the basic information about HIV testing and how it is performed:

## Standard Blood Test:

This was the first HIV antibody test developed and made available, and it is the most widely used. With this test, an initial evaluation is used (the ELISA) and confirmed using a more specific test (the Western Blot). The ELISA test is a blood test specifically used to screen for HIV disease. ELISA stands for Enzyme Linked Immuno Sorbent Assay. This test is not routinely ordered unless there is a suspicion of HIV disease. Results from this test can take up to two weeks to be determined.

## Rapid HIV antibody tests:

Where the standard HIV antibody testing procedure requires up to two weeks for results, the rapid test gives results in five to sixty minutes. For rapid blood testing, the fingertip is cleaned with alcohol and pricked with a lancet to get a small drop of blood. The blood is collected with a specimen loop and transferred to a vial, where it is mixed with a developing solution. For oral testing, oral fluid specimens are obtained by swabbing gums with test devices and placed in a solution. In as little as twenty minutes, the test device will indicate if HIV-1 antibodies are present in the solution.

If HIV-1 antibodies are present, your doctor will immediately suggest further consultation and additional tests. These tests will determine what medications will be right for you. Try to get the facts about HIV/AIDS before you even go in for your tests. Be prepared for whatever the doctor will say.

AIDS is still a major threat, even though newly developed anti-viral drug treatments (called anti-retroviral therapy) have significantly reduced the number of deaths among people with this infection. Drug "cocktails" like Atripla TM and Combivir TM that include protease inhibitors have significantly decreased the AIDS death rate in the US over the last decade.

In June 1981, the first cases of what is now known as AIDS were reported in the USA. During the 1980s, there was a rapid increase in the number of AIDS cases and deaths of people with AIDS. Cases peaked with the 1993 expansion of the case definition, and then declined. The rate of decrease in AIDS diagnoses slowed in the late 1990s. After reaching a plateau, the estimated number of diagnoses has increased slightly each year from 2001. For more information on AIDS statistics, visit http://www.avert. org, a website that claims to be "the world's most popular HIV/AIDS website."

In addition, as reported on the avert.org website, unsafe sex is again on the rise among the gay population, which has a false sense of security because of falling AIDS death rates. Younger men, particularly, are being less and less stringent about using condoms. My own investigation on gay male websites proved that a cavalier attitude about condom protection is prevalent. Epidemiologists expect HIV transmission to increase as a result. In addition, HIV is constantly evolving into new strains. Researchers are diligently developing drugs and therapies to fight these strains as they present themselves.

Remember, my fellow straight spouses, HIV/AIDS is not the only danger to your health. The highly documented rise in sexually transmitted diseases, especially among gay men, is frightening.

Clearly, one of the burdens a straight spouse must bear is her own health, as well as worrying about her gay husband's health. Even if neither of them contracts a dangerous disease, the strain and worry of life is painful. Health risks are multi-layered. They can be pushed away into our subconscious; however, when they surface they create devastating emotional and physical states. My HIV-negative test results brought immediate relief, but for months afterward I woke up at night with anxiety because of the long incubation period of the AIDS virus. While an HIV-positive test for either husband or wife calls for medical and psychological counseling, I am a strong advocate for psychological counseling no matter what the outcome of the test is.

Here is my plea to you: GET TESTED! Go to www. HIVtest.org to find a testing site near you (you may give your name or go anonymously) or go to your women's health clinic. You will find caring individuals there who will not judge you in any way. People who work in health clinics and medical offices do so to help you – not to judge you. It may be scary to go, or you may have the same emotions I had – ANGER, fear and loathing at your gay spouse for putting you in this predicament. Whatever state of mind you are in, go get tested. Then find a therapist.

# 8    WHAT WILL THE NEIGHBORS SAY?

There is NO way to predict to how family, friends, neighbors, work associates, teachers and others in your life will react when they hear that your husband is gay. If you are lucky, as I was, you may have the benefit of family and friends who assemble around you to provide support. Jackie had good friends and neighbors who gave unwavering support. Mary had a wide network of associates from church who stood by her. Many women with gay husbands will not be as lucky. Most close to you, especially family, will become confused and angry over the disclosure of a gay spouse.

In my circumstance, it was the typical "parting of the ways" that happens in most divorces. My family supported me in any way they could. Siblings and friends went into "help Heather" overdrive by calling often and inviting me to visit them for a break of routine. Some friends helped paint my new little house and some invited the kids to sleepovers so I could have a night off. Some took me to lunch and some dropped by just to say hello. Some stayed away, and I have not seen them since. That hurts.

Everyone was curious at first. They asked me all sorts of questions ranging from "How are you going to tell the kids?" to "How could you not have had any idea that your husband was gay?"

At first, I answered as many questions as I could, however, as time passed, I learned to politely deflect those questions. "I'm not really interested in talking about that now... but maybe someday we can have that discussion," became my mantra. My therapist taught me that phrase. I used it a lot. Mary, Carol and Jackie helped assemble the following phases of deflection that they employed:

1. Do you think that I would married him in the first place if I knew he was gay?

2. Do you know everything about your husband?

3. Yes – we had a normal sex life...do you?

4. No, I do not feel stupid for not knowing. Most of us have no idea what is really and honestly going on in our marriages.

5. Yes I feel lost and angry – I guess I feel the same emotions any betrayed spouse feels.

6. We'll figure out a good working relationship for the family. The kids deserve a good and loving relationship with their dad.

7. I understand your curiosity, however these are private matters. Maybe someday I'll feel more comfortable talking to you in detail.

Obviously some of the statements above are meant to cut the discussion off immediately. You will find, however, that some people are so shocked that your husband is gay that they cannot help themselves. They will ask you the most outright questions! It is good to have a few phrases in your arsenal to stop the onslaught.

My husband's family was as shocked as I was when we first told them about his change in sexual orientation. Some of his siblings offered support and stayed as neutral as possible during the year or so before our divorce was final. Of course a few of them separated themselves from us. Most people surrounding the "coming out" of a husband and father are puzzled as to how to react.

To this day, Mary has no idea what her kids' dad told his family about his "coming out." She has never talked about Jeff's infidelity or his homosexuality. She guesses that Jeff's family has no idea of his prior indiscretions. I think my ex-husband's family also has no idea what occurred prior to my becoming aware of his homosexuality. I would guess they know nothing about the details that led to my discovery. We as wives tend to hide these details to insulate our families.

In the year following the disclosure, I was hurt and surprised by his family's lack of contact with me. We were so close before… and after his coming out, they never called to even say hello. Our relationship ended due to his sexual revelation, not because I had changed. I was angry and sad, and terribly disappointed. It was a dark time. People I thought were friends disappeared.

My goal is not to relive the past, but to use it as a means of illustrating how the assistance of a good therapist can help the straight spouse survive. My therapist gave me the tools to move from despair to hope during the challenging time following my husband's disclosure. She assisted in my transformation from wanting to bury my spouse to feeling sorry for him, to not concerning myself with his day-to-day activities except as they relate to our children. My therapist helped me in the darkest hours to find my self-esteem and my courage to carry on. She helped me survive. And I never knew her prior to my need for her.

Until this point in life, I felt as though only the weak needed therapy. No one in my family had ever been to a therapist. Without intention, the underlying family consensus was that shrinks were for the crazy. As far as I knew, no one in my husband's family or mine had ever seen a therapist. My friend suggested that I talk to Joanne.

I called Joanne and talked to her for 45 minutes on the phone. She was kind, she was generous, and she seemed strong – not "counselor wishy-washy." She was business-like. She told me what her background was and what she expected from me if I chose to work with her. We gelled. I chose her over the two other therapists I interviewed. It was a gut feeling.

Joanne counseled me to stand strong. She gave me the tools to work through my husband's issues, and she gave me the tools to protect the kids from my anger and sorrow and disappointment. She taught me how to deal with my despair over the loss of my family, and she gave me exercises that I could do at 4:30 in the morning when I would wake up in a sweat of anxiety and depression. I really think she saved my sanity.

Shortly after the disclosure of my husband's sexuality, Joanne met with both my husband and me. He was in a very regretful phase, and she was wonderful at providing us with a platform for discussion. We only met with her twice, however, because my husband's lawyer counseled him not to give us any ammunition to use against him in a potential future lawsuit. My husband was counseled to quit our joint sessions just as we were making headway on how to approach our divorce. Typical frickin' lawyer.

I must tell you that all was not roses with Joanne. During the roughest times, when I could barely handle all the details of my divorce and was losing my job, I kept missing appointments with Joanne. I became so disorganized that I could not keep track of meetings I had scheduled the day before. One day I told Joanne how I drove straight past her office to my daughter's soccer field. I parked the car, got out and stood by the field for 5 minutes before I could remember where I was supposed to be. Another time I called Joanne in the morning to confirm our noon appointment and then went to lunch with a friend! It was an incredibly stressful time in my life, and Joanne got the brunt of it in the form of missed appointments and overdrawn checks and uncontrolled weeping.

## Discussion:
*How to find a good therapist.*

We all need a good therapist at some time in our lives. If you suspect that your husband is gay and you do not already have a therapist, FIND ONE. I assure you that you won't regret it. Believe me, the emotional rollercoaster that you will ride as you figure out what to do with your marriage, your kids, your friends, your husband and your self-worth will necessitate clear thinking. Relying on friends and family is necessary; however, you will also need the clear and unbiased thinking of someone unrelated to you. And the tools that a therapist possesses to assist you in designing a well-thought-out route to recovery will be worth more than the money you pay her.

If you do not know a good therapist, then be proactive in finding one. Talk to friends. Believe me, you have at least one friend who is seeing a shrink or knows of a good one. Don't be shy. Ask your doctor or clergy or even your tennis pro for a referral! No one needs to know why you are asking. Heck – tell them you are looking for help for your neighbor. If you really do not want to ask friends or associates for a referral, then get on the internet or look in the yellow pages. There should also be categories of specialties like family and marriage counseling, or sexual identity therapy, or even grief counseling. These are usually good types of people to start your search with.

In searching for an appropriate counselor, keep in mind that not all professionals have experience with mixed-orientation couples. Plan on calling a number of potential candidates before you find the one you feel a connection with. Shop carefully for one who is knowledgeable, open, empathetic and fits your personality. Many organizations exist that can help you in your search for a professional counselor, whether private or with governmental or non-profit assistance. I conducted five phone interviews and two face-to-face interviews before choosing Joanne to help me. It may take you even longer. Be patient, if you can. Even though you are at a really rough juncture in life by the time you are looking for therapists, choosing the best one for you will serve you well down the road.

When making your preliminary calls, ask your potential therapist if he/she would be willing to set up a half hour complimentary discussion to see if your needs mesh with his/her specialty. If they will not offer this service, then politely exclude them from your consideration. Any professional therapist who has your best interests in mind should encourage a complimentary interview from you.

A clarification is necessary here. In the previous paragraph I advise potential clients not to hire therapists who do not offer a complimentary discussion. I did not say "consultation." In fact, therapists are actually taught in school and in training not to give complimentary consultations, which are against the therapists' code of ethics according to the American Counselor's Association. This type of session is seriously frowned upon in the profession and considered blatantly unethical, though some practitioners still use this method to attract clients. The "discussion" I refer to above is to help you understand if a therapist's background or expertise is what you are looking for.

During your interviews, ask a few questions that will give you a peek into each therapist's personal bent. Therapists are trained to be objective and to not bring their own beliefs into discussions with a client, however, I can't help but believe that some do. Some questions I asked were:

Have you (the therapist) ever had a client with a homosexual spouse? (A piece of advice here –this is a good time to present which one of the members of the marriage is gay.)

## Additional questions that may be helpful are:

• If so – where is the client in his/her divorce process?

• Have you ever dealt with families with gay members?

• Have you ever worked with infidelity before?

• When counseling couples on marriage therapy, do you tend to help couples stay together or help them adjust to divorce?

• Have you been trained in crisis management?

• Have you worked with children during and after the process of divorce? How about children born to mixed orientation marriages?

• Do you take my insurance?

• Tell each professional a few of the most important or relevant details of your story and choose one that you feel comfortable with. I would like to say that there is some science involved in choosing a therapist, however, my personal belief is that it is mostly instinct. Your gut will tell you when someone is not right for you. Listen to your intuition for clues to compatibility. Don't get too caught up in having to choose the "perfect" therapist. Many clients will change counselors as they proceed through the process of rearranging their lives. Just pick one and get started towards understanding and dealing with the tumultuous landscape of a life that includes a gay husband or a gay ex-husband.

# 9 SHOULD WE TELL THE KIDS?

When a gay husband comes out, everyone involved in his life is thrown on to an emotional rollercoaster. Helping family and friends understand and accept this new reality is a very difficult challenge. Kids add to the predicament, whatever their age. Jackie and Roger chose to tell their kids immediately. Mary, on the other hand, chose to hide it from her children to shield them from pain. Experts agree that this is a wrong approach. Children should be told about their father's homosexuality. The information should be handled with care and delivered in a way that is appropriate for the children's ages. In the end, all children will hear about their gay parent somewhere.

I was fearful that my son would be tormented by kids who would call his dad gay. I lived in fear of putting him on the bus every day because I worried that one of the 6$^{th}$ graders would scream, "Hey everyone – get out of the way for the kid whose dad is a fag!" Don't laugh. This fear paralyzed me. I saw scenes in my head every evening of my sweet little eight-year-old son being teased and tormented by the ugly older kids on the playground. I saw him being shunned from athletic teams because his dad was gay and therefore he must be, too. I cried at least once a day for my poor children who would grow up with a strange family.

It is far better for kids to hear the news from their parents than from outsiders. If your kids are young, they need constant assurance that both parents love them. All divorce publications will say the same thing. Children must first be assured of love and affection from both parents before they can be open to understanding the change between their parents. But children whose parents are divorcing because of a change in sexual orientation can be additionally bewildered. PFLAG suggests a simple and direct statement like, "Mommy and Daddy still love each other and you, but Daddy loves someone else now," or "Mommy and Daddy still love each other and you, but Daddy's love has changed." Small kids can't understand elaborate details about sexuality or homosexuality. They can, however, understand love. And they understand that love through the caring actions their parents demonstrate.

Since most mixed-orientation marriages split, the family breakup creates pain for children no matter what age they are. They may feel varying degrees of abandonment, isolation, insecurity and fear. There is no perfect way to help young people through this experience; however, consistent and open communication and assurances of love from both parents helps.

I encourage you to consider the following guidelines when helping kids of any age work through the crisis:

- Think honestly about what you might say before you say it. Will your words hurt someone? If so, remember the adage "if you don't have something nice to say about someone, then don't say anything at all."

- Use resources (like books, online chat groups and

support groups) to get the facts about homosexuality. Research relevant issues and teach what you learn to people close to you, especially your children.

- As soon as possible, tell the truth to the whole family and support network of friends and supporters. The sooner the truth is revealed, the sooner healing can begin.

- Try not to spread your anger or loathing. Especially try not to encourage homophobia. Speak as honestly as possible without spreading any of your own fear, frustration or judgment.

- Turning your children against their father is a BAD idea. As your children get older they will realize that they were used as emotional pawns. They <u>will</u> turn against those that manipulated them .

A straight spouse can easily become overwhelmed by dealing with the challenges of coping with her children's feelings of loss, pain and betrayal. Don't try to handle this yourself. Seek out professional guidance.

This is a lot of information to absorb, especially if you are about to embark on the daunting task of informing your kids about sexually-oriented changes in your family. Be easy on yourself. We will all make mistakes. My goal with this book is to help you along the very bumpy path of finding balance again, and it is a daunting task. I screwed up numerous times in telling my kids what the heck was changing in our family. The discovery was a mess; the discussion with our kids was a mess…but we made it through, and because we continue to show consistent love for the kids and are open to listening to their fears, we continue to create a balance that is working.

When my husband and I split, our children (who were 8 and 11 at the time) didn't really understand our "talk" with them. We sat them down in his little two-bedroom apartment and told them that from now on they would have two loving homes. We told them that Daddy's feelings

Should We Tell the Kids?

had changed and although he loved them tremendously, and still loved Mommy, he needed to leave our marriage. It was our attempt to "get it right." Looking back, it was a bungled attempt that any psychotherapist would regard as untidy! The message, however, was delivered in a loving, caring way. After both kids heard the news they cried. We all cried together. They knew they would be cared for and safe and loved as Mom and Dad did whatever crazy stuff would come next.

Whether the road in presenting your reality to the kids is smooth or riddled by potholes, always try to be honest and non-judgmental for the sake of the kids. They are your children, but they are also his children. Belittling him will only cause heartache for the kids, as they are as much as part of him as they are of you.

In the beginning, my kids grasped only that Dad had moved into an apartment and that they would have two houses and two different bedrooms. Now that the kids have moved into two homes and the dizzying fog of the breakup has cleared, my daughter has become more accepting of the idea that Mommy desires a man for a life partner, but Daddy does, too. My son has yet to fully understand the situation; however, I feel that he has been somewhat prepared to handle the details that will come when he is older.

One thing that continues to be a challenge for growing children and adolescents is bridging the gap between what they feel and what they have been told in the past. A parent's obligation must include helping kids learn to trust their own feelings and also trust what we as parents tell them. Building a strong foundation of trust in the difficult times following discovery of a gay parent is essential to keep the family foundation from cracking.

If your kids are older, they may be dealing with friends' homophobic attitudes. For kids of this age especially, open communication is really important. Adolescent kids require accurate, direct information and answers to questions. Resentment over family change will almost always surface, and will require increased emotional support and understanding. Children will develop a coping strategy that feels comfortable and safe to them, and will help them deal with what is happening. Some children will take to writing music and excelling at school. Some will act out in negative ways. Each behavior really is concealing deeper issues that they are dealing with. Children need, and often ask for parents to just "be there" for them.

Amity Pierce Buxton, Ph.D, suggests in her book "The Other Side of the Closet – The Coming Out Crisis for Straight Spouses and Families" that parents be honest and open and available as much as possible, even if they are ignored. "Just watch your children and wait," she suggests. Bring the subject up when you can, but not too much. Keep asking if your children want to talk but don't force them to express their feelings. Give them time to process information and let them take baby steps. Once they start talking, let them talk for as long as they want. That is how they think things through. Listen to their feelings, whether you like them or not. Don't judge or be defensive. Dr. Buxon goes on to admit that these requests sound simple but are difficult to fill. She emphasizes that courage is necessary for listening without becoming defensive, to admit mistakes and to change.

In my family, humor is important in maintaining balance. My son is a veritable stand-up comedian. From time to time we tell gay jokes at the dinner table in order to lighten the load of heavy conversation. It works for us and it really helps our family feel close. When we see gay characters on television shows, my son will often make a comment or two about how he wishes his dad would date a guy like that! When possible, it is to everyone's advantage to protect family relationships.

# 10 MOVING ON

A straight wife's initiation into her gay husband's closet is a momentous event. When her husband's private closet door opens and the wife enters, she knows that her life will never be the same again.

It is said that one's true identity is revealed when the going gets tough. My experience with my marriage and the coming out of my husband was the most difficult, traumatic and definitive period of my life. It was the same for the three women who graciously allowed me to tell you their stories in this book. Through their challenges I hope that many women around the world will gain courage to work through the traumatic circumstances that occur when a husband changes his sexual orientation in a marriage.

Writing this book has been a process of defining my new identity. I walked a path of sorrow and anger and fear that was so strong it almost destroyed me. But then something happened. I realized that I was not alone. Many women before me have walked this same path. Some survived the journey with pride and dignity intact. Some were not as fortunate. Here is the path that, although articulated differently in every publication I've read, is generally regarded as the one that leads to the best long term results for women:

## Let go of the past

Spouses need to work through any leftover feelings that could slow their personal growth. They need to stop denying any lingering pain, anger or self-pity. The understanding and acceptance of the death of your old life is necessary for survival. After all, endings are a part of the natural cycle of life. Your old life as a spouse can't be returned to you, but it can be re-made by leaving the painful past behind and choosing only to deal with the future, as uncertain as it is.

It also takes time for spouses to release themselves from their former lives. It is common for spouses to hang onto the old relationship, even after separation or divorce. We as wives will frequently cling to our husbands for security. Carol stayed with Greg for years after knowing in her gut that he was gay. She simply could not cut the ties with him for fear of what would no longer remain in her life.

Then something happens that nudges or forces the spouse to break the ties to her husband. Jackie's catalyst was finding her husband on gay dating websites. Mary's was the fear that she would contract the HIV virus that her husband had been diagnosed with. During those respective moments, the ending became clear. The clouds parted and the sky showed them both the stars they had not "seen" in years.

## Forgive

When I was finally able to let go of my anger towards my husband, my health started to improve, my friends started to call, and my overall life took an upswing. Anger had me so wrapped up in a whirlpool of negativity that for months no one wanted to spend time with me. As soon as I found the most effective resolution of my anger (which was forgiveness), I was then liberated to enjoy my life again.

For me, anger came from judging my husband as uncaring, deceitful and horrible because of the consequences of his coming out. I hated him for the loss of the house I loved. I hated him for my economic instability. I hated him for lying to me and allowing me to live for years believing he was faithful. But did I really understand what he was going through? Did I really understand the complexities of what made him start acting on feelings he may have had, but ignored, for his whole life?

Carol was furious with Greg because he would not let her into his world as he slowly fell into a life of closeted homosexuality. But did Carol really know what fear and anxiety was keeping Greg from living his life with dignity? Did she know his motives for becoming a hermit in their home and removing himself and his wife from the social world of friends and family?

Forgiving a partner allows the spouse to stop struggling to change something that she cannot change. When I decided once and for all to forgive my husband, I felt as though I could accept him as the father of my children, whose actions I no longer had any responsibility for. It set me free. When Mary stopped feeling as though she contributed in any way to her husband's contraction of HIV, it set her free.

A counselor or friend or family member may help you to concentrate on forgiving rather than judging. Boy, is it easy to judgmentally believe that you deserve to hurt or get even with another because he has hurt you. It takes courage and understanding to forgive another. Just the act of saying "I forgive you" to the universe or to your pillow is good enough for many. For me it was stopping my car on the side of the road because I could no longer navigate the vehicle through my tears. I stopped, rolled down the windows and yelled "I fucking forgive you" at the top of my lungs. It wasn't pretty, but it was effective. For me, the act of verbalizing my forgiveness to the wind was enough. It set me free to think of other things and open my heart to new experiences.

For many women, forgiveness is not an easy concept. We want vindication and feel we deserve it. I promise you that the help of a friend, clergy, counselor or family member will bring a balanced picture of your past marriage into focus. It will allow you to see your partner's good qualities and will bring you peace when remembering happy times together. Forgiving does not mean forgetting what happened or naively giving up on the lessons learned from it. The past must be remembered to continue to derive purpose from it. Forgiveness is a release of the past that will allow you to get on with the future.

## Accepting the past as...the past

The sense of loss that straight spouses feel is probably the most profound feeling of the whole coming out process. The loss felt by straight spouses is unique. We often remain vulnerable to feelings because circumstances in our lives keep us in contact with our partners. Caring for children, work and finances may tie us to the man we once loved and loved making love with. Although we may feel continued sexual desire for our partners, we are faced with accepting the reality that a sexual relationship with him is over forever. This feeling of loss of our partner, marriage, personal identity, and dreams is often a straight spouse's greatest pain.

Coming to terms with this loss can be the start of a

new life. I marked the end of my sexual relationship with my spouse by talking to God on a chairlift while skiing in Colorado. I asked him to guide me in cutting the emotional cord that bound me to my spouse. Two days later I returned home and packed away all the items in my house that he had given me as presents. I took all photos of him out of our frames. I stopped writing in the journal I had used when he was with me. I bought a new journal for a new life. For me it was important to mark the end of the past and the beginning of the future.

The act of celebrating a divide between the past and present can be done in any way that suits you. Some women will proclaim it to their pastors. Some will throw away any and everything that reminds them of their spouse. However you find the empowerment that usually accompanies such an act, recognize that the end result you want is to close a door from the past in order to start walking the path of the future.

In her book "The Other Side of the Closet," Dr. Amity Buxton says:

When the past is finally released, there is often a sense of disorientation, but it differs from the confusion felt after the coming out. Although the spouse is still on unfamiliar ground, she now has a stronger sense of self and of personal values. The idea of forging a path through the unknown doesn't seem so daunting.

## Getting over "Why did this happen to me?"

When I was suffering from the devastation my husband left behind when he came out, I wondered "Why did this happen to me?" I was feeling bullied by a force in the universe that I could not understand. My past conditioning led me to believe that I was being punished for doing something wrong. My thoughts, I have learned, are not unique. It took a good deal of time before I was able to discontinue my "poor me" attitude to understand that sooner or later everyone suffers. People get sick. People die. My suffering has come because of the change in sexual orientation of my partner. The choice, I finally understood, was in how I handled it.

By choosing to understand the reality of my situation, I was able to fully grasp and deal with the following truths:

- By hiding his secret from me because he didn't want to "hurt" me, my husband actually devastated me.

- My partner's coming out of the closet was the genesis of him becoming "free." For me it was the beginning of a heartbreaking imprisonment.

- The coming out that was good for him was terrible for me.

All three thoughts demonstrate one overall idea that creates anger for straight wives. What is good for him is bad for me. It is a tough pill to swallow. The coming out of a spouse is terribly destructive for a wife, at least in the short run.

For me, the examination of my experience was the golden light at the end of my tunnel. When I finally was able to ask myself "What good can I derive from this terrible experience?" I got the idea to write this book.

## Soul searching

For **Jackie**, finding a personal connection with a new religion provided an anchor for her fears. **Mary** left behind her religion and searched for her soul in the outdoors. She found a deep and rewarding connection with her spirit by planting flowers and trees. Today she has a lovely garden where she spends a great deal of time. **Carol** found solace by connecting with her family. After Greg died she became the aunt that she always wanted to be. She took care of her nieces and nephews regularly and basked in the warmth of a family who was anxious to support her.

My search for "completeness" led me to read all kinds of books like "The Secret" which states that, *Without exception, every human being has the ability to transform any weakness or suffering into strength, power, perfect peace, health, and abundance.*

I read everything I could about Eastern religions, karma and personal empowerment. I attended seminars on achieving happiness and tranquility.

I felt driven by a force to explore the healing words of Tony Robbins. I took the ideas of mentors that gave me peace and combined it with the traditional ideas of my Christian faith. I created a comfort zone in my mind that allowed me to heal. This is a common occurrence for people who are hit by a traumatic experience like the coming out of a spouse. By taking bits and pieces of varying spiritual paths, many pave their own road to acceptance.

We all found meaning for our suffering in different ways and with different spiritual dimensions. For all of us, the search for new meaning in our lives brought considerable insights. In the emptiness of our pain we all found glimmers of meaning that we may not have seen had we not felt the devastation.

I remember feeling the touch of a spiritual connection to a force in the universe I could not explain. All the straight spouses I have spoken with over the years have mentioned the spiritual dimension as a critical part of their transformation to healing and acceptance.

## Starting over

Eventually the healing process for a straight wife proceeds to a point where she can shift her focus from the past, to the present, to the future. Through releasing the past and starting over with new ideas and beliefs, the spouse has changed her previous patterns of thinking. Her ideas about her role in the world, about relationships, and about marriage have certainly changed.

Partners from the marriage will surely envision a new life. My ex-husband, who never previously donated time to charitable organizations, is now a full-fledged contributor to Meals on Wheels. Lately he has donated a significant amount of money to PFLAG and other related organizations, and last summer he rode his bike from Minneapolis to Chicago to raise awareness of HIV/AIDS-related charities.

After Mary and Jeff parted ways, he joined the local YMCA and donated his free time to help HIV-infected men keep their strength. She eventually quit her job at the office building where she had worked for 15 years and took a class on becoming a pit manager at the local casino. Today Mary enjoys a flexible schedule to parent her two lovely children and she cherishes the opportunity to meet all kinds of different people at the black jack tables.

Shortly after Greg died (without ever revealing his homosexuality), Carol joined a women's organization that helps immigrant families. She also became very involved in the lives of her siblings' families.

After the dust settled on my divorce, I wanted to feel the winter wind on my cheeks. I got a home equity loan and fulfilled a raging desire to snow ski. I spent the season skiing at as many local ski areas as possible. I quit a job I hated and started one where I earned half as much money but had the free time to write a book.

Dreaming of a new life and new possibilities allows many of us to survive the catastrophe of the coming out of our spouse. Dreaming and actually making our wishes happen, however, require completely different skills. Many of us will hesitate to create a new life out of fear of failure. But finally, at the bottom of it all, there is really nothing to fear. You have been through a lot. But hopefully you now have the tools for a new life to begin.

## The lessons I learned:

During the years since my divorce I have added broad faith in a wide spectrum of spirituality to my original faith. While I realize that my path has no end point, I realize finally that my life is better now. I am healthier now. I am stronger now. It has been a very bumpy road, but I am grateful for the journey and for the authentic lives that are emerging for my ex-husband and me.

In her book "My Husband Is Gay," Carol Grever offers the following list of lessons she learned in her journey to discovery, anger, fear, acceptance and recovery:

- Living a lie is hell.

- There are no accidents. We somehow choose the events of our lives in order to learn what our spirits need. Everything is a teacher for those who are awake.

- People may not love you the way you'd choose, but that does not mean that they don't love you with all they have.

- "No one is ever, always fortunate." (Euripides, in The Trojan Women)

- We have the right to be angry sometimes, but that doesn't give us the right to be cruel.

- Accepting what is makes it possible to let go of what can't change.

- The greatest power is to create change in your own life.

- By intentionally changing negative thought patterns, we can heal emotional wounds.

- All spirit is one and we are intrinsically connected to all beings.

- Finally, I know that I have everything I need to live the life I choose.

The day that I found out about my husband's change from straight to gay seems so long ago. It has been a terrible, lonely, wonderful, eye-opening journey. I wrote three complete renditions of this book as a form of therapy. The first rendition was so full of anger and hurt that my editor told me to take a half year off and start again. I took a year off. And another. It is amazing the personal transformation that occurs in a couple of years. The final draft of this book was written in joy – for my new life and the lives of my children and their father.

Thornton Wilder said, "We can only be said to be alive in those moments when our hearts are conscious of our treasures."

Today I choose to be alive and aware of the joy in my life.